Coding for Teens
Minecraft® & Lua
Intermediate Guide
with 162
awesome Activities

An unofficial Minecraft® Book

Mark A. Morrison

Turtles have prepared the first task for you: name them

1.

2.

3.

Contents

Your ideas

Introduction

Hello, and welcome!

This book is a self-contained class that helps with self-teaching programming in the Lua language, using Minecraft with the ComputerCraftEdu mod. The book is meant for Teens over 11 years old and older, as well as anyone who would like to learn the basics of programming in a quick and fun way. You will learn how to write programs in the Lua language using Code Editor. An easier visual editor is explained in my first book **Coding for Kids: Minecraft® & Lua. Beginner's Guide with 127 awesome Activities An unofficial Minecraft® Book.**

You will also get to know all the basic elements utilized in all programming languages. A wonderful adventure awaits you. Let's begin!

```
for n = 1, 6 do
turtle.placeDown()
turtle.forward()
end
turtle.select(2)
turtle.placeDown()
```

Your ideas

Chapter 2: Installing the necessary components

What will you need?

- A computer with internet access
- Java
- A Minecraft Java Edition account
- The ComputerCraftEdu mod
- Forge

Let's start with installing all the components we need.

Attention:

The instructions are for Windows but can be easily adapted for other operating systems.

Installing Java

Let's start by checking whether you have Java installed already. Open the start menu and type in control panel.

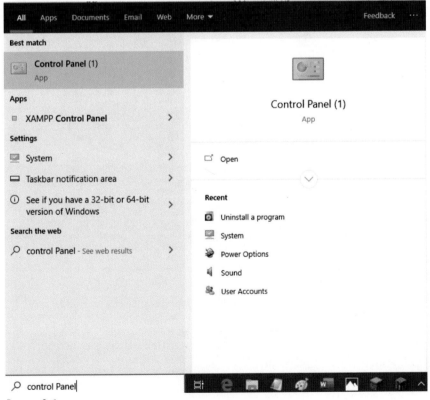

Image 2.1

Open the control panel.

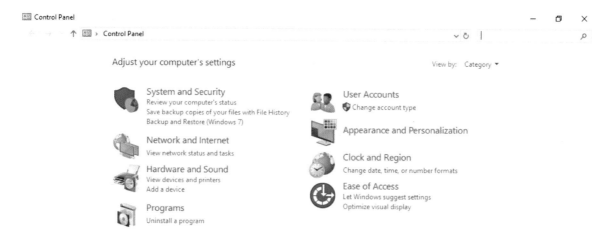

Image 2.2

Select Uninstall a program and check whether Java is installed.

If it is, you will see it on the list.

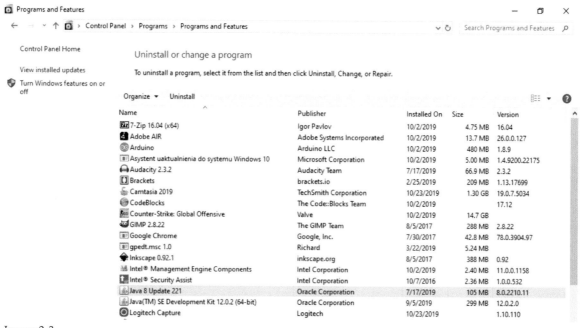

Image 2.3

If you already have Java installed, go to the next part. If not, install it.

To install Java, you will need to go online and type 'Java runtime' into Google. Enter the website, and then download Java version 8.

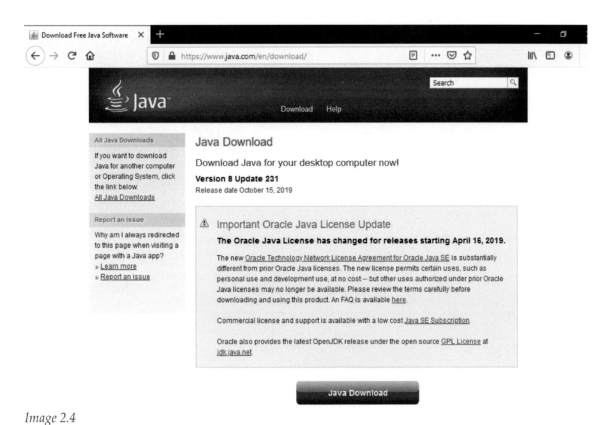

Image 2.4

Agree to all the terms and conditions and the download will start.

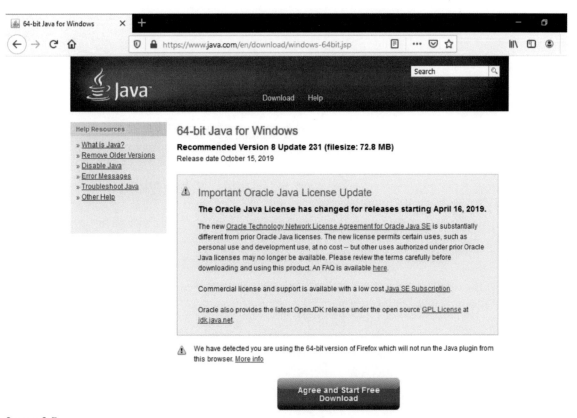

Image 2.5

Open the installation file and click Install.

The Java installer will download automatically. You will need to wait a moment. After the download, the installer will launch automatically.

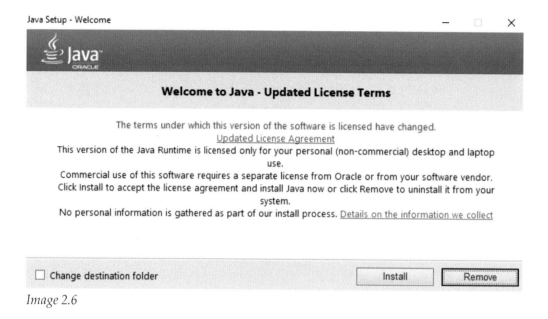

Image 2.6

The Java installation will now proceed. Wait a moment, then click on close, and that's it, Java is already installed.

Buying and installing Minecraft

Remember, you will need to complete this step together with a parent.

If you already have Minecraft, you can skip this step. If you don't, you will need to buy the game. To buy Minecraft, go to the *http://minecraft.net/*.

You will need to click the big, green BUY MINECRAFT JAVA EDITION (PC AND MAC) button.

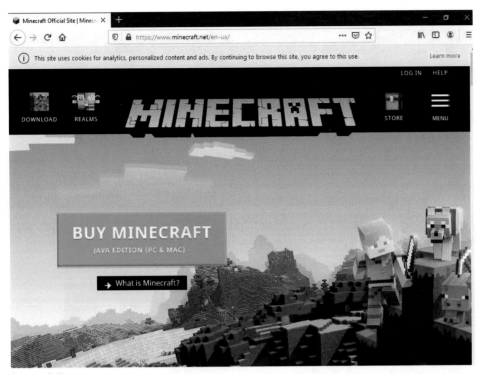

Image 2.7

Then you will need to fill out a form.

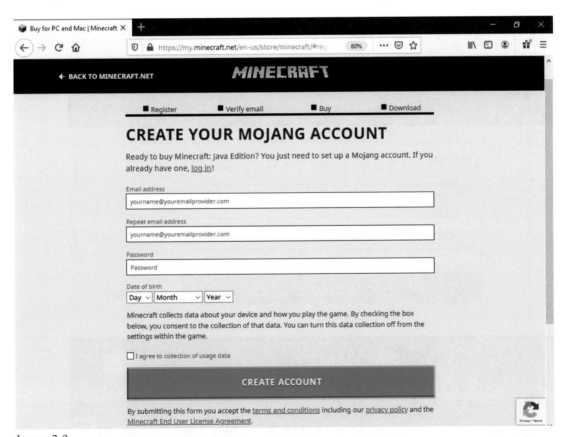

Image 2.8

Agree and press the create account button. Then you will need to go to your inbox to get the verification code. Copy it from the e-mail you got from Mojang, paste it into the website and click the verify button.

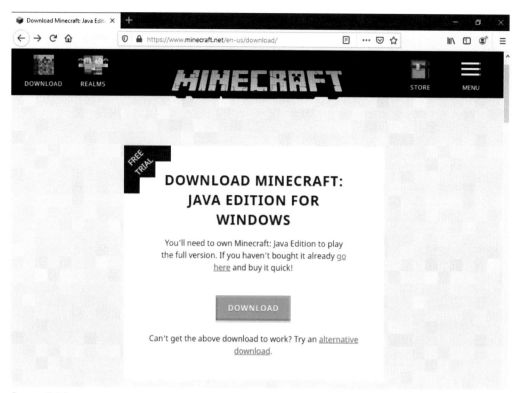

Image 2.13

Installation for other operating systems is similar, you just need to select an alternative download.

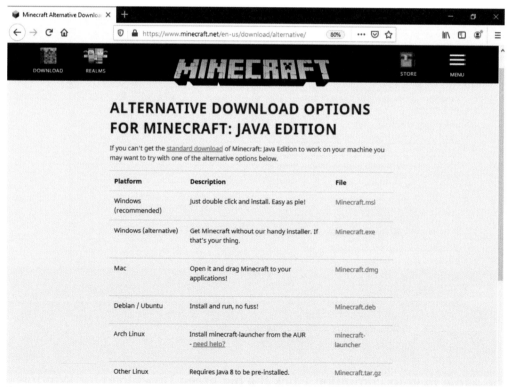

Image 2.14

Open the launcher installer.

Image 2.15

Choose the installation path that interests you, then click Next and Install.

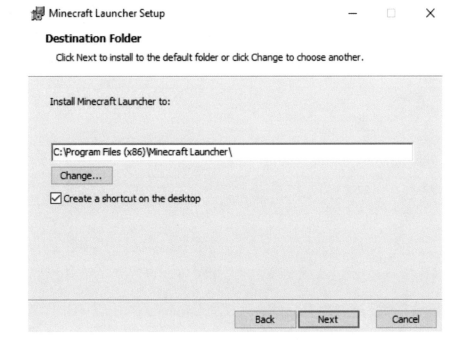

Image 2.16

Minecraft Launcher Setup   — □ ✕

Ready to install Minecraft Launcher

Click Install to begin the installation. Click Back to review or change any of your installation settings. Click Cancel to exit the wizard.

Back   🛡Install   Cancel

Image 2.17

Confirm the administrator permissions and click Finish.

Minecraft Launcher Setup   — □ ✕

Completed the Minecraft Launcher Setup Wizard

Click the Finish button to exit the Setup Wizard.

☑ Start Minecraft after closing the installer

Back   Finish   Cancel

Image 2.18

he Forge tool

l need Forge. To download it, go to the
raftforge.net website.

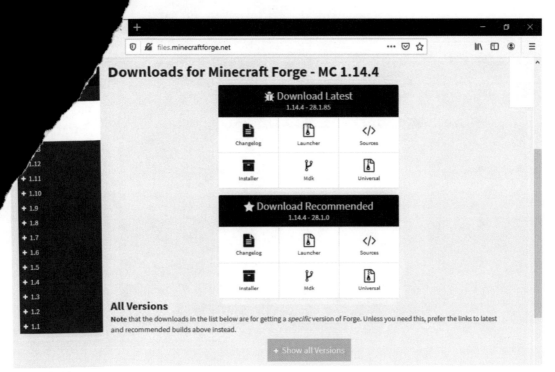

Image 2.19

Choose Version 1.8.9 from the menu on the left. Download the installer by clicking on the Windows Installer.

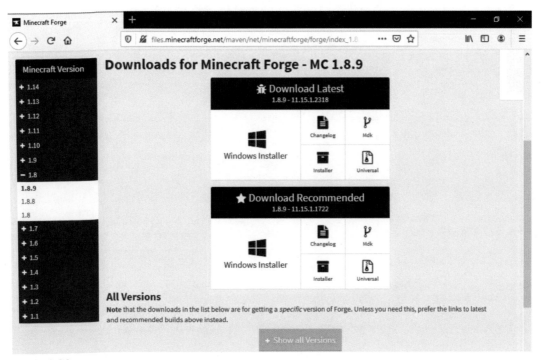

Image 2.20

On the next site, you will have to click SKIP after viewing th[...]
installer. An installation window will pop up – you don't need t[...]
here, just click OK.

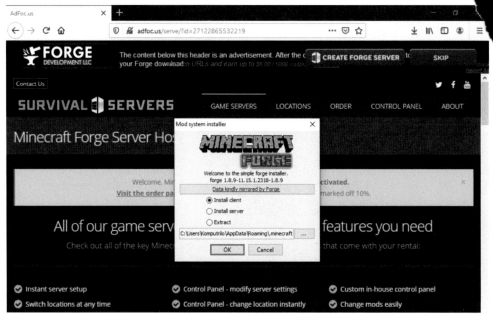

Image 2.21

For Mac OS, you will have to download the installer, and then open a file. If the system won't allow that, you will have to go to System Preferences, and then to Security & Privacy. At the "forge..." message, click "Open Anyway".

Image 2.22

Image 2.23

The program will unzip into the Minecraft files, confirm with OK.

Now you can launch Minecraft. After launch, your version of Forge should automatically be visible at the version list.

Installation of the ComputerCraftEdu mod

To do programming, you will need the ComputerCraftEdu game modification. To install it, go to the http://computercraftedu.com/ website.

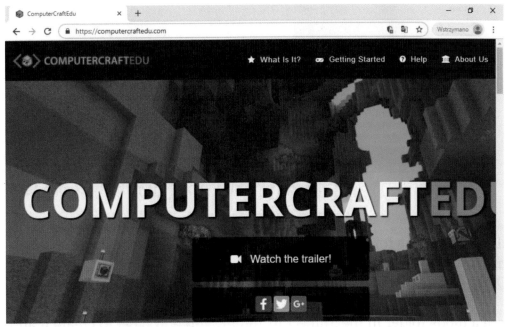

Image 2.24

Equipment

Another important thing in Minecraft is your equipment. How to open it and what do you need it for?

The equipment is used to store blocks and items. Because you're playing on the Creative Mode, you will access all blocks in the game after opening the equipment.

Us̶ ̶he E key to open your equipment.

̶ block, drag it into one of your slots at the bottom of the screen. You place ̶ ̶o u̶sing your right mou̶se button (RMB) and de̶stroy using the left ̶3). To place or destroy a block, you need to be close enough from ̶e at it (the block will be marked by a black frame).

̶ut your mouse over it. Now place:

̶ ̶b̶l̶o̶c̶k̶s̶ of granite (to grab more than one bloc̶l, click LMB. To t̶a̶k̶e̶ ̶a̶ ̶w̶h̶o̶l̶e̶ ̶s̶t̶a̶c̶k̶, meaning 64 blocks, press Shift+LMB on the block)
- 3 blocks of watermelon (to find this block, you need to drag the slider or scroll down)
You can destroy all blocks now.

Meet the turtles

The most important character during your programming adventure will be… the turtle! You're going to program the turtle to obey our commands and solve tasks.
To place the turtle down in your world, open your equipment by pressing E. You will find the turtle in the second tab, after clicking the right arrow in the upper right corner.

Image 3.5

Now change the game mode to creative.
To do that, click the Game Mode button, enough times to make Game Mode: Creative appear.
Now name the world with your name, and then click Create New World.

Image 3.4

Moving Around the Minecraft world

To move around the world, you will have to use the following keys: W – forward, S- backward, A- left, D- right. The mouse plays a very important part, allowing you to look around. The mouse wheel changes the selected slot.

To jump, press space. Creative mode also allows you to fly. You need to double press space to do that. To go back down, use the Shift key, or double press space again.

Time for some exercises in Minecraft. Do the following:
- 3 steps forward
- 2 steps left
- 4 steps right
- 1 steps backward
- 5 jumps
- Fly up
- And go back to the ground.

Equipment

Another important thing in Minecraft is your equipment. How to open it and what do you need it for?

The equipment is used to store blocks and items. Because you're playing on the Creative Mode, you will access all blocks in the game after opening the equipment.

Use the E key to open your equipment.

To select a block, drag it into one of your slots at the bottom of the screen. You place the blocks in game using your right mouse button (RMB) and destroy using the left mouse button (LMB). To place or destroy a block, you need to be close enough from it and aim your mouse at it (the block will be marked by a black frame).

To see the block name, put your mouse over it. Now place:
- 1 block of glass
- 2 blocks of granite (to grab more than one block, click LMB. To take a whole stack, meaning 64 blocks, press Shift+LMB on the block)
- 3 blocks of watermelon (to find this block, you need to drag the slider or scroll down)
You can destroy all blocks now.

Meet the turtles

The most important character during your programming adventure will be... the turtle! You're going to program the turtle to obey our commands and solve tasks.

To place the turtle down in your world, open your equipment by pressing E. You will find the turtle in the second tab, after clicking the right arrow in the upper right corner.

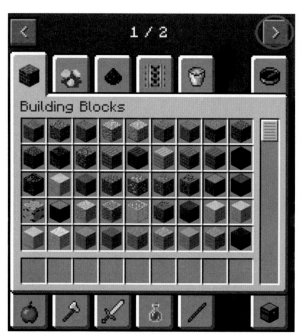

Image 3.5

Click the remote icon to find the turtle.

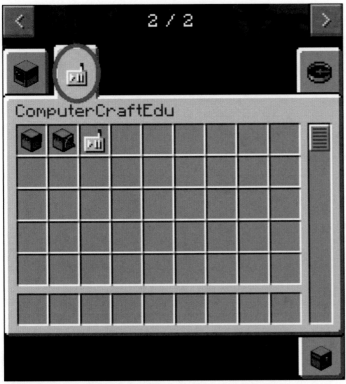

Image 3.6

Drag the turtle and the remote onto the equipment slots on the bottom.

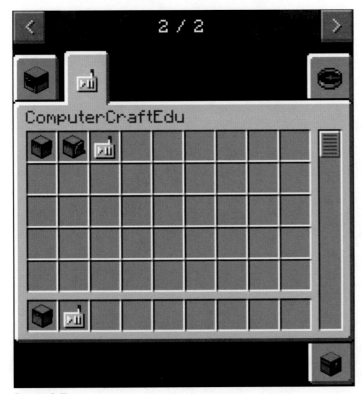

Image 3.7

To program the turtle, you will have to put the remote in your right hand. To do that, exit your equipment (by pressing either Escape or E), and select the remote slot by using your mouse wheel. The active slot is the one with the bold frame. Then press RMB.

Image 3.8

Image 3.9

Now select the turtle slot and place down the turtle. The game treats the turtle as a regular block, so use RMB to place it.

Go 3 blocks up and try to set the turtle in front of you.

As you can see, you can't place the turtle in the air, the same as other blocks.

Now put it on the ground.

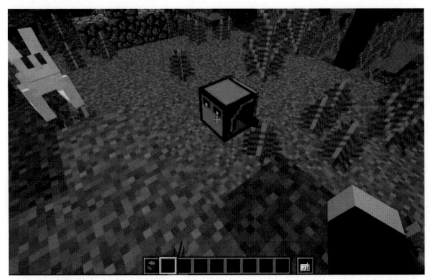

Image 3.10

The most important element used to control the turtle is the remote. Thanks to the remote, you can access the turtle's interface. To open it, point the cursor at the turtle and press RMB.

You will find 4 tabs in the interface:

- Program – programming the turtle. There are two modes: visual (you are using it), and text.
- Customize – change the name and look of your turtle.
- Inventory – the inventory of your turtle.
- Remote – directly controlling the turtle.

Image 3.11

Exercise 1

You will learn to change the look and name of your turtle.

To do that, go to the Customize tab, and then change the look using arrows. To change the nickname of your turtle, delete the default one using the Backspace key and write your chosen name there.

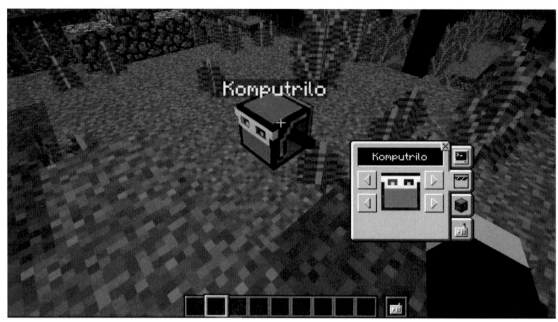

Image 3.12

Chapter 4: Text programming and movement functions

In this book, you'll learn the Lua language, which is perfect for learning programming.
In the first part of our book, we utilized the visual editor. In the following chapters, you will learn to utilize the code editor. It may seem harder than the visual one, but it's important to learn it because it gives you many more options.

Look at the visual editor. In the top right corner, the turtle will provide tips about some functions that you may use.

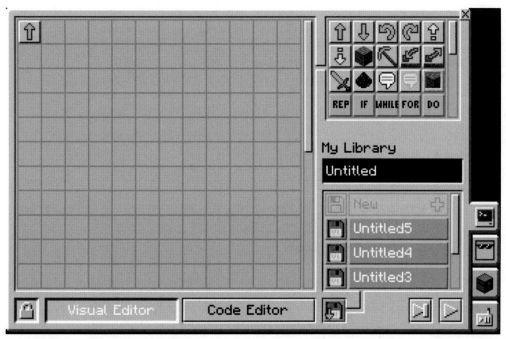

Image 4.1

Can you guess, which picture is responsible for:
- Walking forward?
- Walking up?
- Digging?
- Placing blocks?

If you remember, great! A nice start with text programming, the same kind as professional programmers do every day, awaits you.

Look at the program below, written in the visual editor. The turtle will walk forward here.

Launch the program using the button marked.

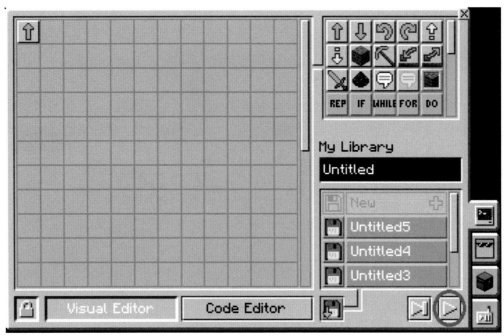

Image 4.2

The turtle walked forward, executing the program written in the visual editor.

Code editor

To go to the code editor, press the Code Editor button.

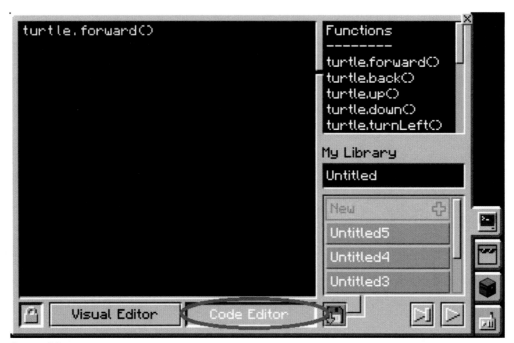

Image 4.3

If you want to go back to the visual editor, press the Visual Editor button.

The code editor allows much more freedom when writing programs.
On the right, you'll see names of some of the functions you can put into the editor.

The functions use the word turtle, followed by the function name, ex. forward.

Look at the list of functions you can use.

Image 4.4

The turtle.forward() function

Let's take a look at the turtle.forward() function. It allows the turtle to move forward.

It's composed of several elements, as shown in the picture below.

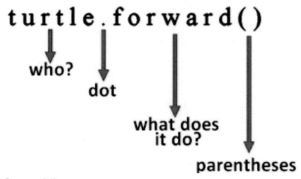

Image 4.5

In this book, we'll use those names: turtle, variable, function, while keeping in mind that they are simplified names. Professionals would use different names.

Image 4.6

There are also other commands, starting with turtleedu. It's like that, because the education mod of the turtle (ComputerCraftEdu) uses another modification, called ComputerCraft. ComputerCraft also has turtles, with functions starting with turtle. In the educational version, several functions were added, and those start with turtleedu.

One of those functions is turtleedu.say(), which you will learn in the following chapters. Keep in mind, that the function in the screenshot below has an argument between the brackets - the word "Hello!".

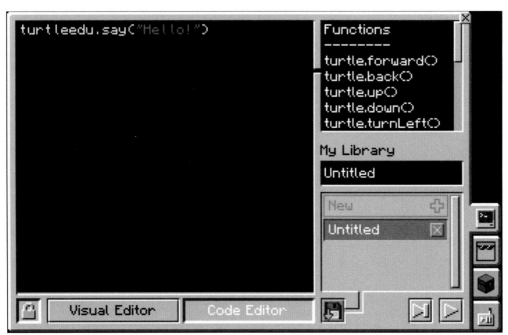

Image 4.7

To learn programming, you have to exercise writing commands using your keyboard. The more programs you write, the easier it'll be for you to spot and understand problems.

Exercise 2

Using the text editor, write a program that will make the turtle walk three steps forward.

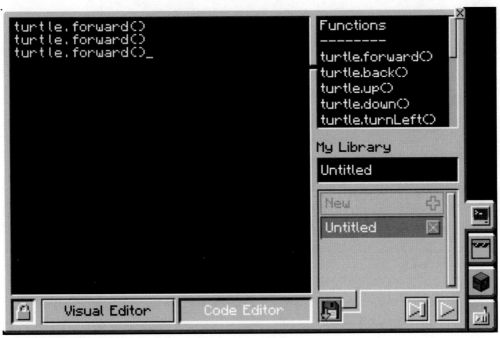

Image 4.8

If you're not sure whether you did it correctly, you can go back to the text editor for a moment. Keep in mind, that the function is named Move Forward.

Image 4.9

The turtle.back() function and the turtle suggestions

What do you think about the turtle.back() function is for? This function makes the turtle take one step back.

Now you will learn how to make programming simpler using the TAB key. At the end of the last program, add first letters of our command, "tu".

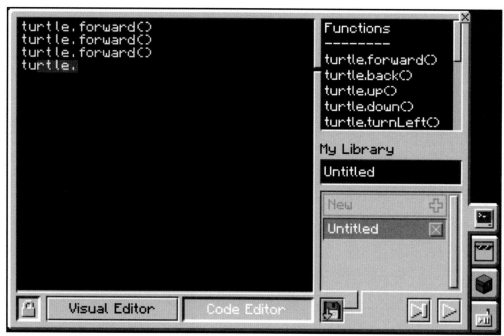

Image 4.10

The turtle suggests that you can write "turtle". That's exactly what you need to put there if you want the turtle to go back. That's why you should press the TAB key at this moment.

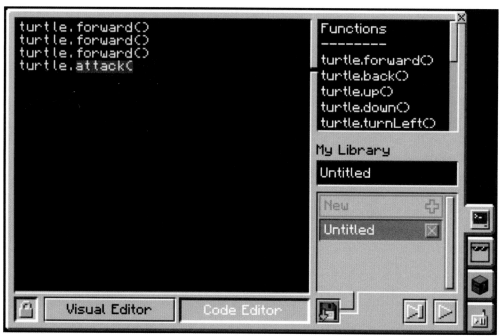

Image 4.11

The turtle finished the code fragment for you and suggests what to do next. You want the turtle to select the back() function now. You can type it in manually, starting with the letter b, and then selecting TAB, or you can use keyboard arrows. If you scroll using up or down arrows, the turtle will suggest more functions that can be used in this place in the code. Try to find the back() function that way and confirm with TAB.

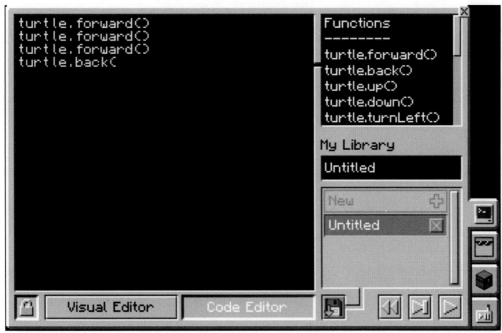

Image 4.12

Remember that every function has brackets at the end. Function arguments may be put into those brackets.

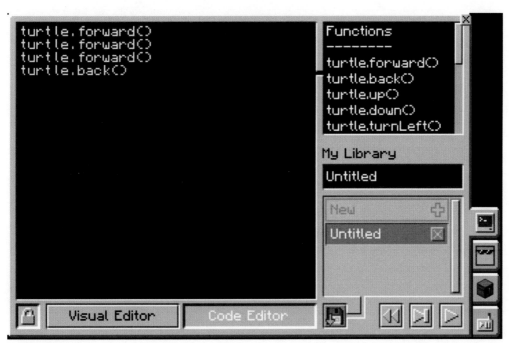

Image 4.13

Exercise 3

Finish the previous program so that the turtle goes back to the starting position after the three steps forward.

Check if you did it correctly.

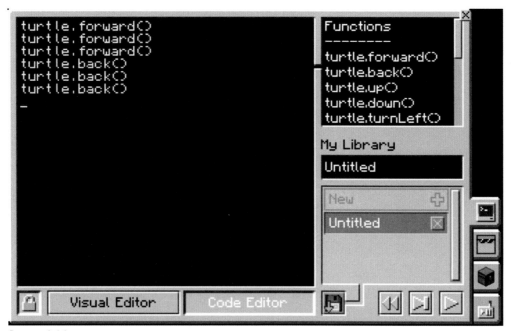

Image 4.14

The turtle.up() and turtle.down() functions

Look at the function list on the right and try to figure out, which function will tell the turtle to go up?

The turtle.up() function tells the turtle to go up.
To go down, use the turtle.down() function.

Exercise 4

Write a program that will make the turtle jump, so first go up, and then down.

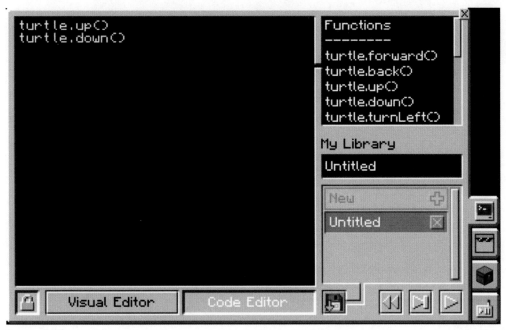

Image 4.15

Exercise 5

Build a column for the turtle, as in the image below, and put the turtle at the bottom of it.

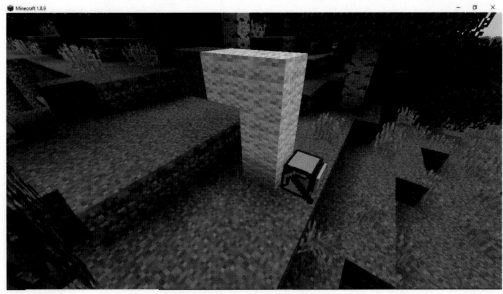

Image 4.16

Now write a program that will make the turtle go up the column and stand on the last, red wool block.

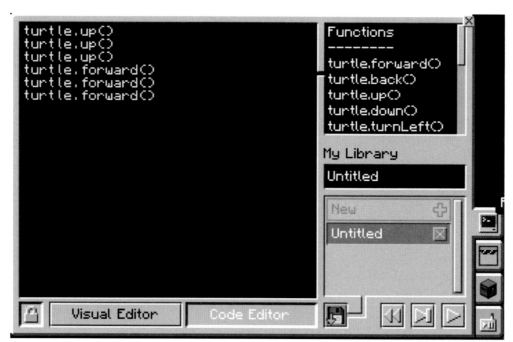

Image 4.17

Image 4.18

Exercise 6

Build a wall with a hole for the turtle, as shown in the image below.

Image 4.19

Write a program that will make the turtle go through the hole to the other side.

The turtle.turnLeft() and turtle.turnRight() functions

What direction can the turtle turn in? Right or left. That means we need to tell it to turn left or turn right.

You will now learn functions that will allow you to turn the turtle.

If you looked at the function list, you already know we mean the turtle.turnLeft() and turtle.turnRight() functions.

You've probably noticed that the second part of the function name starts with a great letter. It's done so because you use great letters when function names contain multiple words. That makes the function name more easy to read.

Exercise 7

Let's write a program together. It'll make the turtle turn right four times.

Image 4.20

Exercise 8

Build two bookshelves for the turtle, as in the image below.

Image 4.21

Write a program that will make the turtle go from one bookshelf to the other, to take a look at it up close.

Exercise 9
Dig a ditch as shown in the image below.

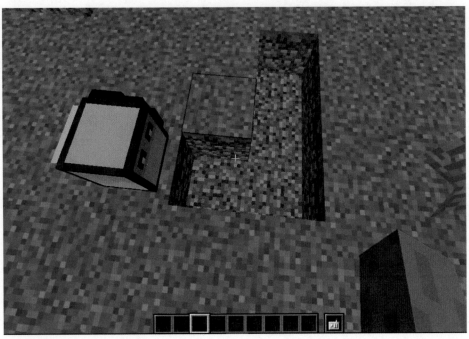

Image 4.22

Pour lava at the end of the ditch. The lava will form a nice little pool in the ditch. You probably know that lava pours "around" on flat ground, but when you pour it next to a lowered area, it'll go into that.

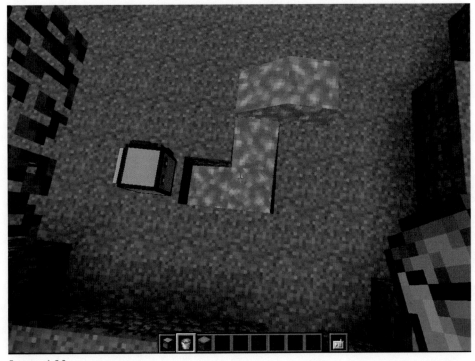

Image 4.23

Now take a while and try to figure out what moves will the turtle have to take to go over the lava pool and enter the source at the end of it.

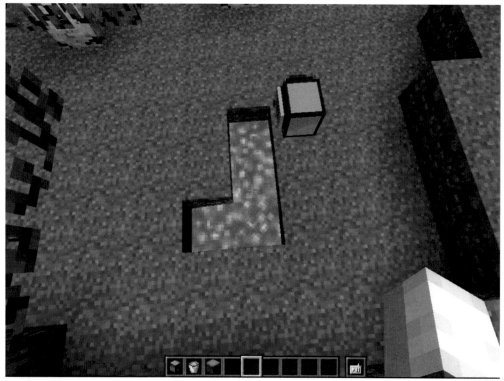

Image 4.24

Exercise 10
Write a program that will make the turtle execute each one of the functions below once. Keep in mind, this task has many possible solutions.

- turtle.forward()
- turtle.back()
- turtle.up()
- turtle.down()
- turtle.turnLeft()
- turtle.turnRight()

Chapter 5: Digging

Since you already know how to move the turtle around, time to grab a pickaxe and go down into the mines. But before you do that, you need to learn how to dig.

The turtle.dig() function

The digging function is turtle.dig(). Try it out on a torch.

Exercise 11

Place a torch in front of the turtle.

Image 5.1

Let's write a program together to make the turtle dig that torch.

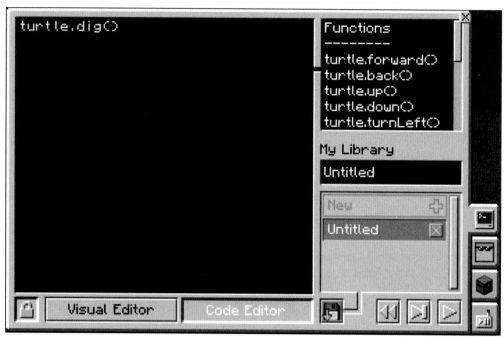

Image 5.2

Exercise 12

Put 3 blocks of wool in various colors in front of the turtle: red, orange, and green.

Image 5.3

Write a program that will make the turtle dig those blocks.

Exercise 13

Build an obstacle course for the turtle as in the image below.

Image 5.4

Write a program that will make the turtle take part in a hurdling race, but instead of jumping over them, it destroys them until it reaches the finish line.

Image 5.5

Exercise 14
Write a program that will make the turtle complete the obstacle course without destroying the fences. It can be a simplified version that will make the turtle fly over all the obstacles.

Exercise 15
Build blocks around the turtle with Cracked Stone Bricks as in the image below.

Image 5.6

Write a program that will make the turtle destroy every brick around itself.

The turtle.digUp() and turtle.digDown()

The turtle can dig in various directions:
- in front of itself,
- above itself,
- below itself.

You already know that to dig forward, you need to use the turtle.dig() command.

You can also specify the directions by adding words Up on Down at the end of the function name, before the brackets.

The turtle.digUp() function is used to make the turtle dig up.
The turtle.digDown() function is used to make the turtle dig down.

Let's try them out in a few exercises.

Exercise 16

Build a tower of colored glass pane blocks, as in the image below. To place a block on the turtle, you have to do it while sneaking (default: hold left shift key).

Image 5.7

Write a program that will make the turtle destroy all glass panes in order.

Exercise 17
Build a glowstone block path and place the turtle at the start of the path.

Image 5.8

Write a program that will make the turtle turn off the lights by destroying all glowstone blocks.

Image 5.9

Exercise 18

Find a piece of flat land for the turtle.

Change 3 blocks in front of it into podzol, as in the image below.

Image 5.10

Write a program that will make the turtle dig up the podzol blocks that do not fit the terrain.

Image 5.11

Exercise 19
Build a + sign out of ice blocks in front of the ice.

Image 5.12

Write a program that will make the turtle dig up only the block of ice from the middle.

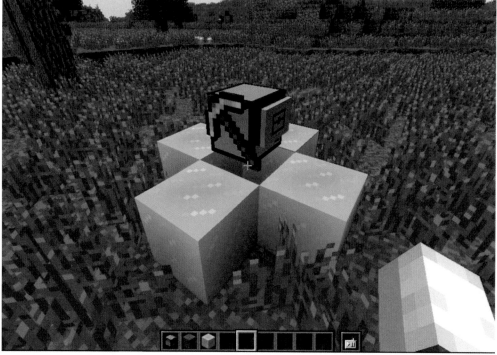

Image 5.13

Chapter 6: The builder turtle

The turtle's inventory

Do you think the turtle has its own inventory? Yes, it does.

To get to it, you'll have to use the Inventory tab. Do you think you can find the destroyed block of ice from the previous task there? Of course not, because that blocks never gives you ice as an item.

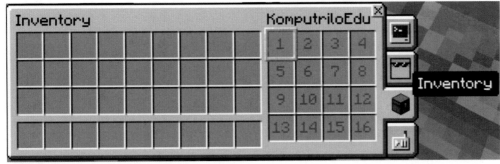

Image 6.1

Exercise 20
Place the turtle in front of a tree.

Image 6.2

Write a program that will make the turtle collect two blocks of wood. Check the solution at the end of the book.

In which slot of the turtle's inventory did the wood appear? In the first empty slot, of course.

Do you know what the bold frame in the inventory means? It means that a slot is active. The same as in your inventory.

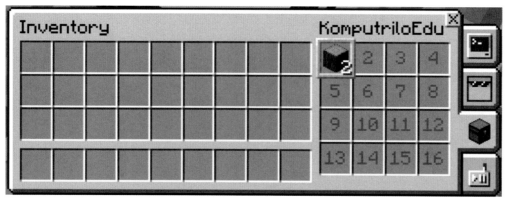

Image 6.3

Interesting fact.
Do you know what happens if you play Minecraft with a full inventory and try to collect blocks? Nothing, they won't fit in a full inventory.

Now undo the previous wood program. To do that, click the double left arrow key as shown in the image below.

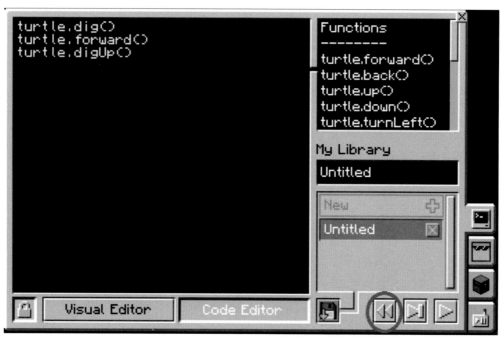

Image 6.4

Fill the turtle's inventory with string.

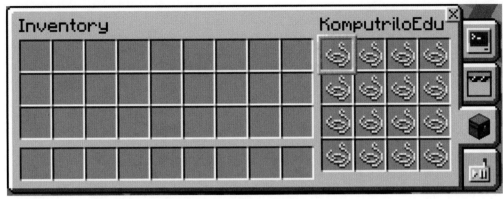

Image 6.5

What will happen to the logs if you run the program again?
They're spilled in the world!

Image 6.6

The turtle.place() function

The turtle can jump, dance, and destroy blocks. Now it's time to build something.

Can you find the name of the function to place blocks? If you looked at the function list, you probably already know that the function is called turtle.place().

Exercise 21

For example, let's write a program that will make the turtle place a crafting table - the basic survival tool in Minecraft.

Stop and think for a bit: what slot do you need to put the block in to make the turtle place it? As you probably remember, the first one, the default active slot.

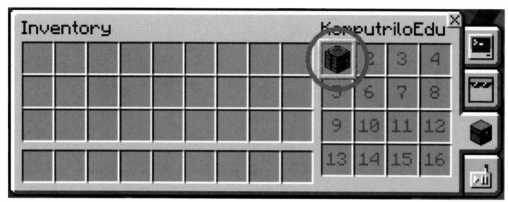

Image 6.7

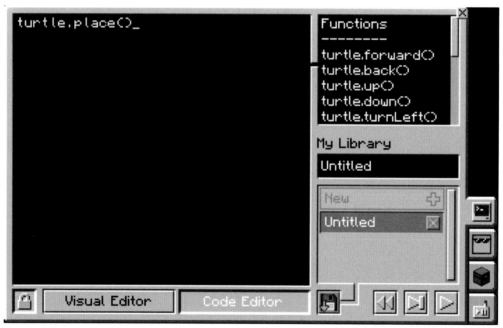

Image 6.8

Exercise 22

Write a program that will make the turtle build a tower out of three green clay blocks.

Image 6.9

Exercise 23

Put two blocks of gold in the turtle's inventory.

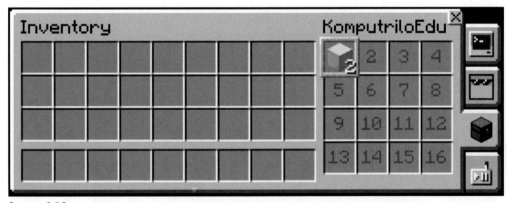

Image 6.10

Build two constructions as in the picture below and place the turtle on top of one of them.

Image 6.11

Write a program that will make the turtle first place a block of gold in the middle of the first construction, and then the second one in the middle of the second construction.

Image 6.12

The turtle.placeDown() function

Do you remember the directions the turtle could dig in? As a reminder, the turtle can dig:

- in front of itself,
- over itself,
- under itself.

It can place blocks in those same directions.

If digging down is turtle.digDown(), do you think you know what will the placing blocks down function be called?

It's called turtle.placeDown().

Exercise 24

Let's write a program that will make the turtle put down three watermelons under itself, using the turtle.placeDown() function.

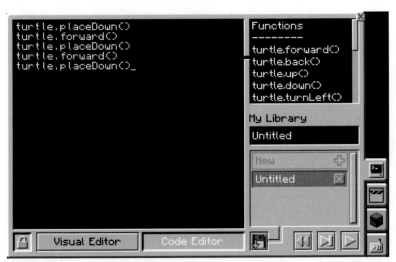

Image 6.13

Image 6.14

The turtle.placeUp() function

To make the turtle place blocks above itself, you need to use the turtle.placeUp() function.

Exercise 25
Write a program that will make the turtle, alternately, place a block on its' head and then destroy it.

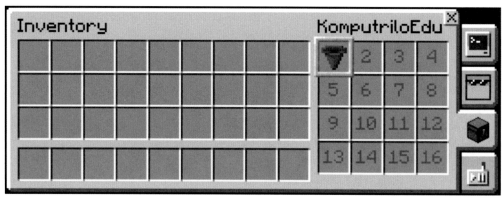

Image 6.15

Exercise 26
Using sponge blocks, build an "o" shaped mark for the turtle and place the turtle above it.

Image 6.16

Write a program that will make the turtle go around over every block of sponge.

Exercise 27
Modify the previous program so that the turtle builds a cobblestone wall on each
sponge block.

Exercise 6.17

Exercise 28
Place a block of TNT under the turtle, and then write a program that will make the
turtle light that block up.

Do you know what function you should use to make the turtle light up the block
when it holds flint and steel? The turtle.place() function of course.

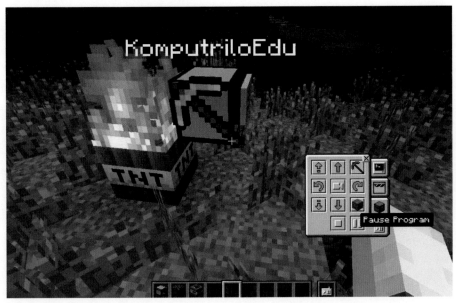

Image 6.18

Exercise 29
Build two holes as in the image shown. Put a block of hay in one of them.

Image 6.19

Write a program that will make the turtle dig the block up from one hole and put it in the other.

Chapter 7: Slot changing and comments

Your task now will be to instruct the turtle to build a 4 block tower, placing oak and spruce wood alternately, so it looks like this:

Image 7.1

Now think how to do it with one program.

The turtle.select() function

To do it, you'll have to use the turtle.select(n) function, where n will be the slot number.
Do you know which slot will be active after running the program below?

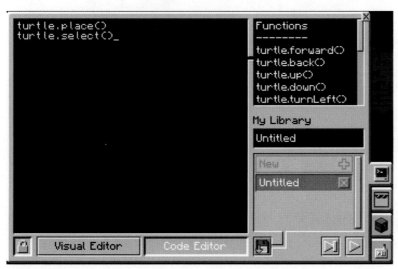

Image 7.2

You might guess, but you don't really know! That's why we have the brackets. You need to put arguments the function needs between them. So if you want to change the active slot to the second one, you need to put 2 in the brackets. Do that and try to place two different blocks on top of each other.

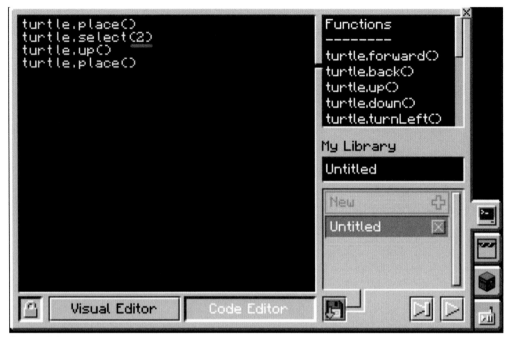

Image 7.3

Image 7.4

Exercise 30
Now finish the task so that the turtle places two missing tower blocks.

Exercise 31
Write a program that will make the turtle build stairs 5 blocks tall, but you have to use 3 different glass colors - red, blue, and green.

Image 7.5

Exercise 32
Build a small farm as shown in the picture.

Image 7.6

Write a program that will make the turtle plant two carrots and two potatoes.
Do you know how to make the crops go faster so that you can check if the turtle did
the task properly? You will need a bonemeal. Use it on the crops by clicking the right
mouse button.

Image 7.7

Exercise 33

Place 3 diamond ore blocks in front of the turtle.

Image 7.8

What slot will all the diamonds end up in? As you can probably figure out, the first slot, if it's the currently active slot.

Can you do anything to make the turtle place one diamond in 3 different slots each? Of course, you have to change the active slot during digging.

Write a program that will make the turtle collect the diamonds so that every diamond ends up in a different inventory slot.

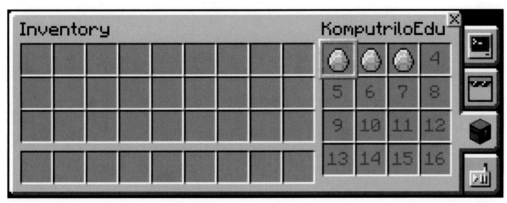

Image 7.9

Exercise 34

Place an acacia plank block, an item frame, and a sword in the turtle's inventory. Write a program that will make the turtle place the plank block, then place the item frame on it, and then put the sword in it (use the turtle.place() function).

Image 7.10

Comments

You can add comments in the editor by writing after the double "--" symbol.

Let's describe the previous program using comments.

What should be included in the slot to ensure the program works properly? Let's explain it using the comments.

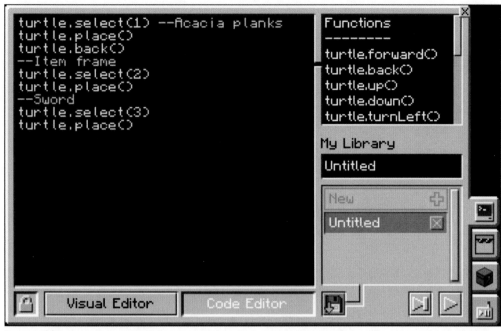

Image 7.11

Do the comments impact the program in any way? Of course not, they're only there to improve how the code reads. Thanks to the comments, you know what is where.

Exercise 35

Look at the comments below. Try to write a program they describe.

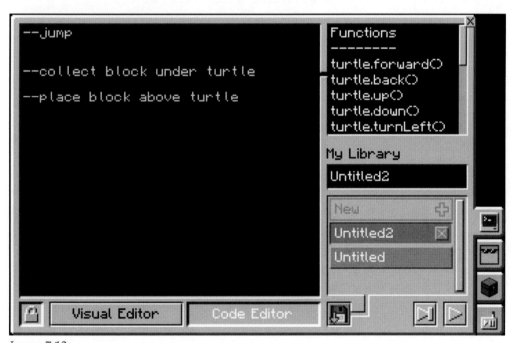

Image 7.12

Exercise 36

Write a program that will make the turtle build a wall out of five leaf blocks, and then set one of them on fire using flint and steel. Add a comment in the place where you change the active slot to the flit and steel one.

Image 7.13

Chapter 8: Repeating

The Repeat instruction (visual editor)

And now a small surprise: go to the visual editor for a moment. Let's write a program using the Repeat instruction in the visual editor.

The Repeat instruction will repeat everything that's contained within it, a set number of times. For example, the "I will bite on this cookie" is done once, but REP 5 "I will bite a cookie" means I'll bite it five times.

You need to remember that everything has a beginning and an end. That's why you need to write REP 5 DO ... END and the code you want to repeat is contained between DO and END. For example, make the turtle jump five times. Yellow arrows are commands to move up and down.

Image 8.1

You can read it like this:

REP: repeat 5 times
DO: do this action (up, down)
END: end repeating

When you put in the REP instruction alone, you will see red fields, and the program won't work.
Why? Because it lacks something.

Image 8.2

After choosing the first red field, possible elements that you can put in there will be displayed. To put a number there, look for the Number command. Then the red field will display further elements that can be put there. Let's choose DO. The last red field only allows for the END word, so put that in.

Fill in the red fields to create five repetitions. For now, don't put anything between DO and END.

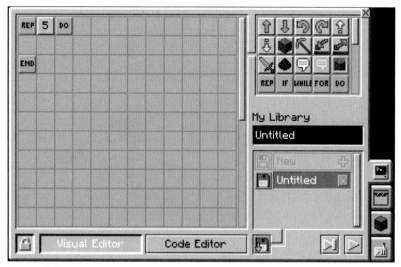

Image 8.3

The for loop

Now you will learn about the for loop.

It gives you much more control than the REP statement from the visual editor. For now, you'll learn the simpler form that will allow you to repeat fragments of a program. Switch to code editor.

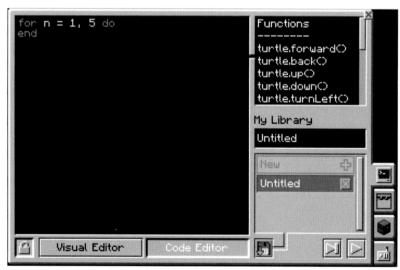

Image 8.4

Now you can see how the REP statement looks in the code editor and, surprise - it turned into the for loop.

The <u>for</u> loop is always executed <u>for something</u>.

Draw five anvils here and assign them numbers from 1 to 5.

You have five anvils, so after for, you will write n (the anvil number) = 1, 5. That means that the for loop will consider anvils 1 to 5.

Now think: what will the for loop do when you write for n = 1, 8? It will consider anvils numbered 1 to 8, and in a more advanced wording, it will execute for n = 1 to 8.

Between do and end you have to write commands for what you want the turtle to do. Let's put a comment there for now.

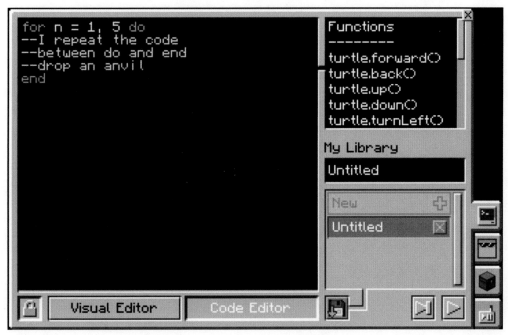

Image 8.5

Exercise 37

Dig a hole five blocks deep and pour water into it. Put five anvils into the turtle's inventory.

Image 8.6

Let's write a program that will make the turtle throw five anvils into the water-filled hole. Use the for variable for it.

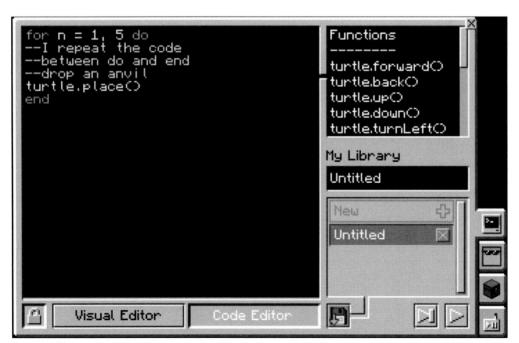

Image 8.7

The hole is now filled in.

Image 8.8

Exercise 38

Look at the program below and answer some questions.

1. How many times will the turtle go forward?
2. How many times will the turtle place a block?
3. How many times will the turtle go up?
4. What should you change to make the turtle go forward and up six times?

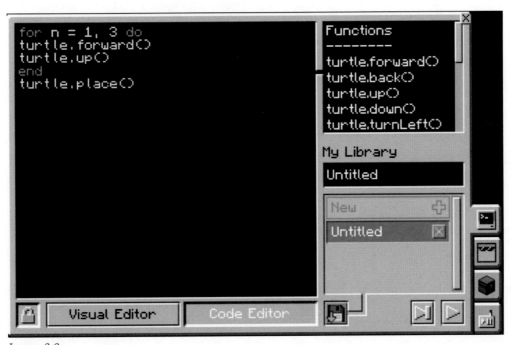

Image 8.9

Exercise 39

Write a program with a for loop that will make the turtle destroy and place a torch alternately ten times.

Exercise 40

Write a program that will make the turtle build a wall out of 15 brick blocks.

Image 8.10

Exercise 41
Build a square for the turtle on the ground, as in the image below.

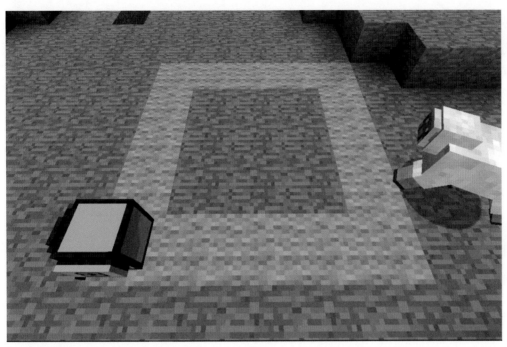

Image 8.11

Let's write a program with the for loop. It will make the turtle go around this square in a circle twenty five times.

Attention! There's a trap in this exercise because the turtle will repeat four steps (three times forward, and turn right) to go over the square once. So to calculate what to put into the for loop in such a program, you need to multiply 25 times 4.

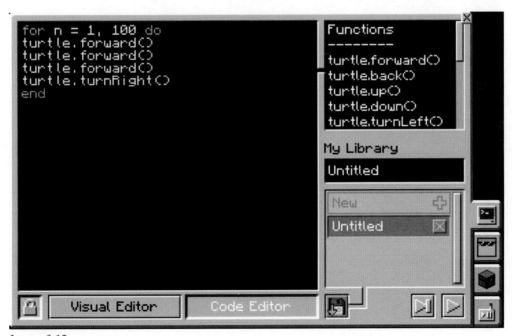

Image 8.12

You can also write this program differently, making the turtle repeat going around the whole square twenty five times.

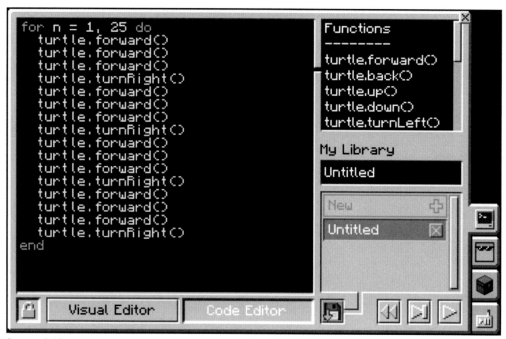

Image 8.13

This exercise can also be solved by embedding one for loop in another one.

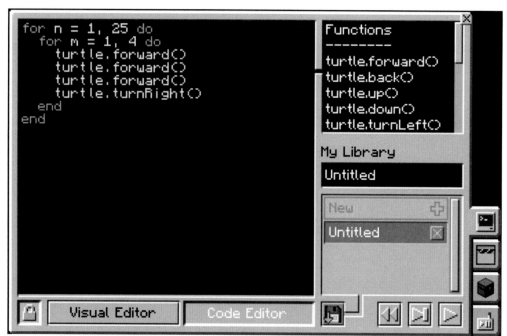

Image 8.14

Remember that one task can sometimes have multiple solutions.

Exercise 42

Write a program that will make the turtle place sixty four sheep from three blocks high.

Image 8.15

Exercise 43

Write a program that will make the turtle turn around ten times and then walk forward once. Add comments that will indicate what functions are repeated and what functions aren't.

Remember, you can still write code after the end statement, it won't be repeated by the for loop!

Exercise 44

Write a program that will make the turtle place six Jack o'Lanterns next to one another and then place one regular pumpkin at the end.

Image 8.16

Exercise 45

Write a program that will make the turtle build a redstone tower eight blocks high, and put a lamp on top. Use the for loop.

Image 8.17

Chapter 9: The use of chat by the turtle, and variables

The turtleedu.say() function

Our educational turtle is special, that's why it can speak. The turtleedu.say() function is an addition created specifically for the educational turtle. Calling it is a bit different than with the other function. Instead of turtle, you need to put turtleedu in.

But how can it know what should it say? That's what the argument is for – the space between brackets. You can put a number or some text there.

Let's command the turtle to say the number five.

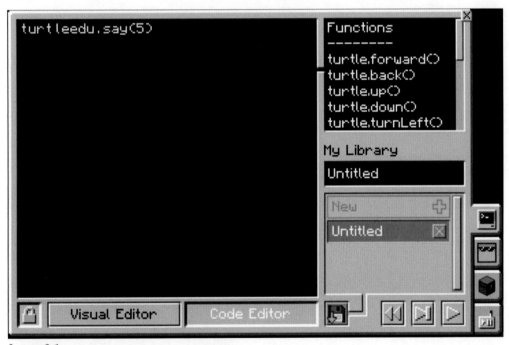

Image 9.1

Image 9.2

The turtle can also speak words.

Think what's your favorite school item. If you already know, command the turtle to say it. But remember, the text isn't the same as numbers. When coding, you need to put text in quotation marks, and if you do it properly, the turtle will highlight it red.

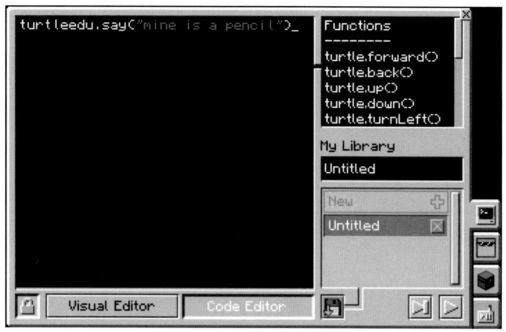

Image 9.3

Exercise 46
Write a program that will make the turtle put red, yellow, and orange carpet on its head alternately and say their colors each time.

Image 9.4

Exercise 47

Write a program that will make the turtle do at least four moves imitating dancing ten times. During the program execution, the turtle should repeat "hello, hello" and "I am pretty" in the chat.

Variables

Our turtle can also say what's in a variable.

Using the variables, the turtle can remember various data. That data can be numbers, text, and many other things. Depending on what's in a variable, it can be a variable of a given data type. We'll focus on the two first types mentioned above. Let's start with the numbers.

Number variables

Take a piece of paper and write the number five on it. Say aloud what number is on the paper. Now hide it. Can you say, without looking, what number is written down on the paper? Five, of course you remember it.

Now take the same piece of paper and cross out the number written before, and write the number seven next to it. Can you still say the last written number without looking?

A variable is like a piece of paper for the turtle. You can have multiple variables in a program, that's why they need to have names. Using variables, the turtle can remember numbers and use them later.

The = character assigns value to a variable.

Exercise 48

Let's write a program that will teach the turtle then the variable called number is equal to 10. You can call variables however you want, it's just a name.

The turtle should then say what's the value of the variable.

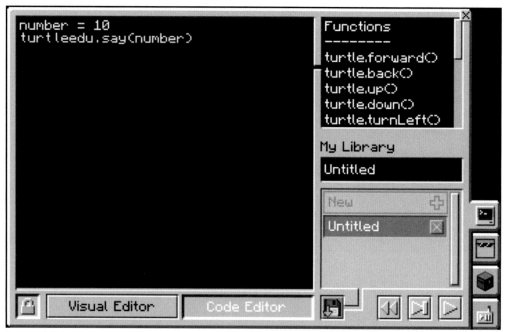

```
number = 10
turtleedu.say(number)
```

Functions
----
turtle.forward()
turtle.back()
turtle.up()
turtle.down()
turtle.turnLeft()

My Library

Untitled

New

Untitled

Visual Editor   Code Editor

Image 9.5

Our smart turtle has said what is the value of the variable correctly.

[KomputriloEdu] 10

Image 9.6

Changing values

Let's create a variable called A of value 6.

A = 6

Now you can increase its value by ex. Two, using the + sign.

Do you know how much is A+2? It's 6+2, so 8.

To permanently increase the value of A, you need to write it like this:

A = A+2

We added 2 to the A variable, equal to 6 at the start, and then we assigned that new value to the variable.

Exercise 49
Calculate and write the final value of each variable in the table.

X = 3 X = X + 1	
Y = 4 Y = Y + Y	
Z = X + Y	
W = 9 W = W - 3	
W = W - X	
X = 3 + 1 X = X * 2	

Exercise 50
Look at the program below and think – what will the turtle say for each line?

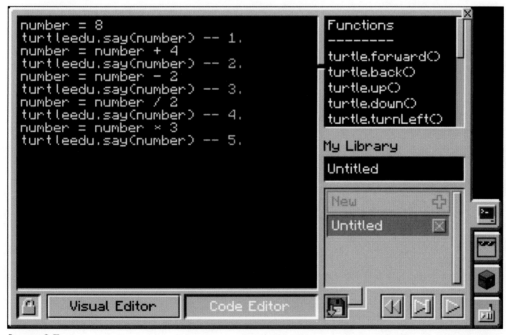

Image 9.7

Exercise 51

Let's write a program that will make the turtle remember a variable of x equal to 1 and say what is x in the chat.

Image 9.8

Image 9.9

Now let's modify the previous program so that the turtle repeats the variable value ten times.

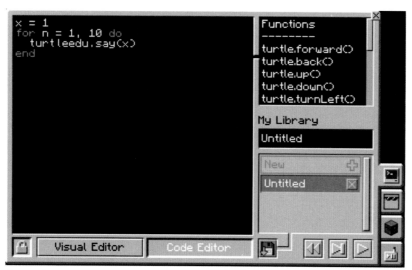

Image 9.10

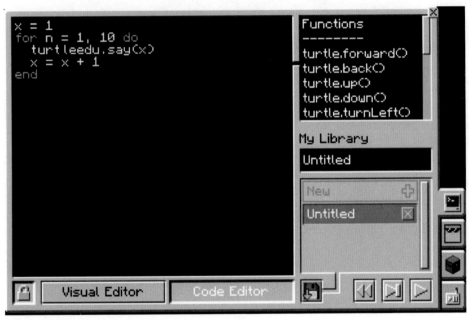

```
[KomputriloEdu] 1
[KomputriloEdu] 1
[KomputriloEdu] 1
[KomputriloEdu] 1
[KomputriloEdu] 1
[KomputriloEdu] 1
[KomputriloEdu] 1
[KomputriloEdu] 1
[KomputriloEdu] 1
[KomputriloEdu] 1
```

Image 9.11

Let's make the turtle say something else than 1 over and over again. Let's add a code to the loop that will increase x by 1 with every loop.

```
x = 1
for n = 1, 10 do
    turtleedu.say(x)
    x = x + 1
end
```

Functions
----
turtle.forward()
turtle.back()
turtle.up()
turtle.down()
turtle.turnLeft()

My Library

Untitled

New

Untitled

Visual Editor   Code Editor

Image 9.12

```
[KomputriloEdu] 1
[KomputriloEdu] 2
[KomputriloEdu] 3
[KomputriloEdu] 4
[KomputriloEdu] 5
[KomputriloEdu] 6
[KomputriloEdu] 7
[KomputriloEdu] 8
[KomputriloEdu] 9
[KomputriloEdu] 10
```

Image 9.13

Exercise 52
Write a program that will make the turtle count down from 20 to 1.

Exercise 53
Write a program that will make the turtle dig a ditch three blocks long and say how many blocks it has dug up already after every block. Set the countdown using a variable called blocks.

Image 9.14

Exercise 54

Let's create two variables called water and lava. Assign slot numbers to them, and put a water bucked and a lava bucket in the appropriate slots.

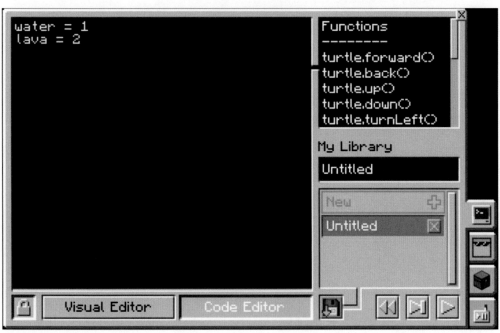

Image 9.15

Now select the water slot using variables, and pour water under the turtle. Then select the lava slot and pour lava down under the turtle? What will be created when we combine lava and water? Obsidian.

Image 9.16

Variables can be texts too

Take a new piece of paper and write the name of your favorite food on it. Then hide the paper. Can you still tell, without looking, what's on it? Yes, because we can remember texts. The turtle can store text in variables.

What will the turtle say now?

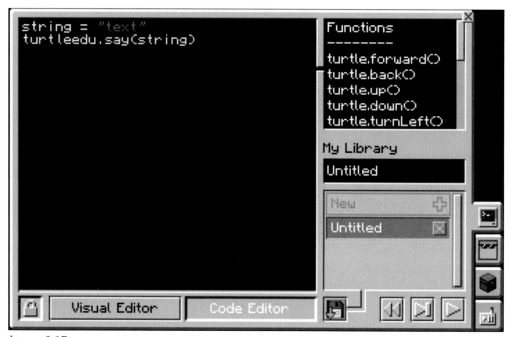

Image 9.17

Of course, the turtle will say "text", because that's what the string variable is storing.

Image 9.18

Exercise 55

Let's now create a variable called x that will store the text "candy". Command the turtle to say what the variable contains, and then let's teach it that the x variable is now the number twelve. Make the turtle say what's in the variable a second time.

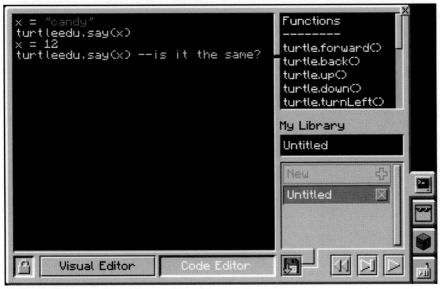

Image 9.19

The x variable is a text at the start and then turns into a number.

Image 9.20

Keep in mind that in the Lua programming language, variables can first be text, and then numbers. So the data type of a variable can change during the program execution.

Exercise 56

Write a program that will make the turtle assign the string "Woof woof" to the w (for wolf) variable.

Then it should display it in chat twenty times.

Image 9.21

Variables in the for loop

We managed to write programs that will make the turtle count down, but we never did it in the simplest possible way.

We have a surprise for you. When you put n=1, 20 into the for loop, what we're really doing is creating a variable that the for loop will increase from 1 to 20 by 1 for every repeat of the loop. That's why you can now write a program that will make the turtle count up from 1 to 100 in a much simpler way.

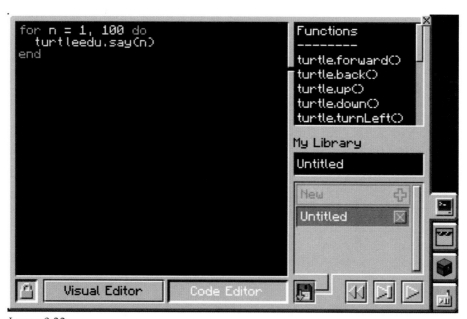

Image 9.22

Interesting fact – you don't need to use n in the for loop. It can be called whatever you want, just like with other variables.

Instead of n, let's write potato in the for loop. To do that, remove n from the program and put in your own name. You have to do it both in the for loop and in the function, as shown in the image below.

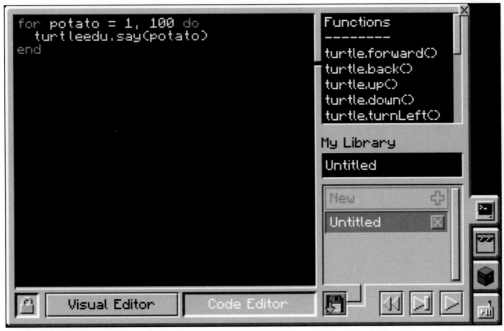

Image 9.23

Exercise 57
Write a program that will make the turtle count from 1 to 16 on the n variable, but always say double the n value in the chat. To multiply, use the * sign.

Will the values the turtle say be odd or even? You probably already know they'll be even because we multiply by 2.

Exercise 58
Build a ten blocks long redstone ore wall for the turtle as in the image below.

Image 9.24

Write a program that will make the turtle collect those blocks, but change the slot to a different one each time.

Will every redstone ore block yield the same amount of redstone? See for yourself.

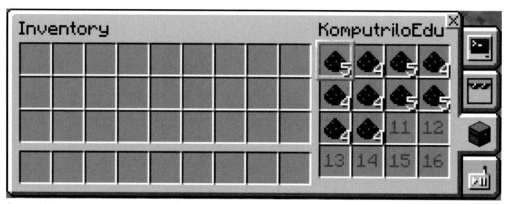

Image 9.25

Exercise 59

Put all sixteen wool colors in the turtle's inventory.

Note: You can quickly transfer items to proper player slots using number keys on the top of your keyboard.

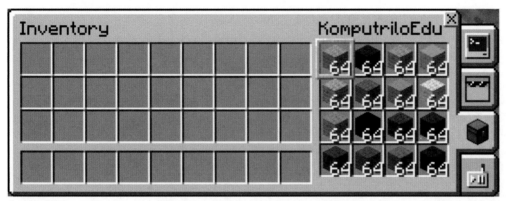

Image 9.26

Now write a program that will make the turtle build a tower 16 blocks high, but using a different wool color for every level.

Image 9.27

True or False

You know what true and false mean, right? Variables can also have those values.

True and false are reserved words for true and false values, and cannot be variable names. The editor marks them green.

Exercise 60

Let's write a program that will make the turtle assign true to the variable x and false to the variable y. Then it should say the values stored in those variables.

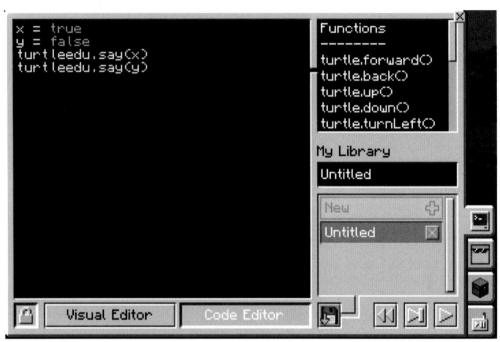

Image 9.28

Image 9.29

Exercise 61

Let's write a program. It should make the turtle remember the HW variable as false.
In the program, the turtle should do this, in order:

- Say "I've done my homework?"
- Say the HW variable value.
- Say "Wait a moment".
- Change the value of HW
- to true
- And say "I did it".

And say the variable value again.

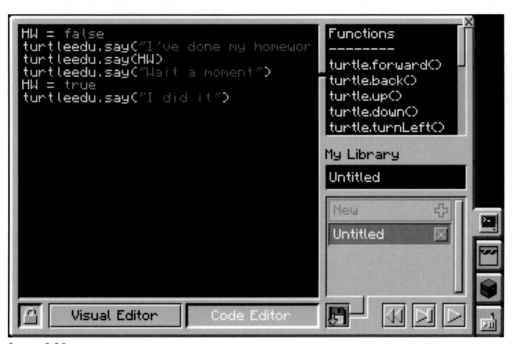

Image 9.30

Chapter 10: Conditional statements

Comparison operands

You can compare the numbers. For that, you will use various signs (operands). Let's take a look at them.

Do you know what they mean in math?

= equal
≠ not equal
< less than
> more than
⩽ less or equal to
⩾ more or equal to

Keep in mind that before we used the = sign to assign values to variables. In the visual editor, the same sign is used to compare two values, but in text editor, == is used to do that.

Exercise 62

Look at the expressions below and try to decide whether they're true or false. Put TRUE or FALSE next to each expression in the table. Compare your solutions with the answers at the end of the book.

6 < 2	
10 = 4	
6 = 6	
6 > 3	
3 ≠ 3	

Can you see the difference between ⩽ and <? The first one has an additional line, which allows for the numbers being equal.

9 ≤ 11	TRUE
11 ≤ 8	FALSE
6 > 6	FALSE
3 ≥ 3	TRUE

When you want to compare two values in a program, use the == sign.

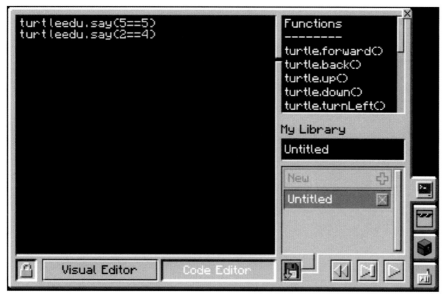

Image 10.1

The turtle said which expression is true and which is false.

[KomputriloEdu] true
[KomputriloEdu] false

Image 10.2

If you want to check if both values are not equal, you need to put in tilde and equal signs: "~=".

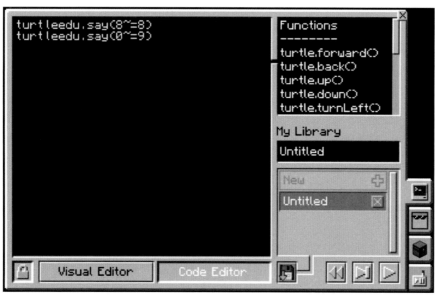

Image 10.3

[KomputriloEdu] false
[KomputriloEdu] true

Image 10.4

To use the ≥ sign, you need to type in ">=". For ≤, you type in ">=".

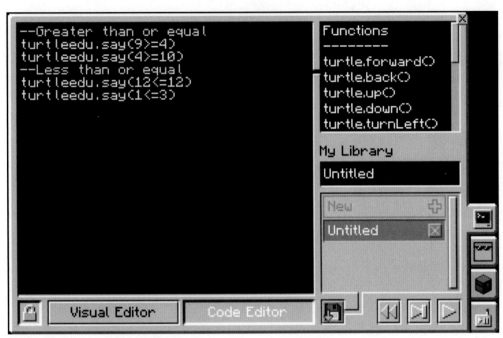

Image 10.5

Image 10.6

The "<" and ">" signs look the same in the code editor.

Exercise 63

Let's write a program that will make the turtle say whether:

- 6>3 is true or false;
- 7 < 7 is true or false;
- 8 ≤ 8 is true or false;
- 3 + 3 = 6 is true or false;
- 9 ≠ 8 is true or false.

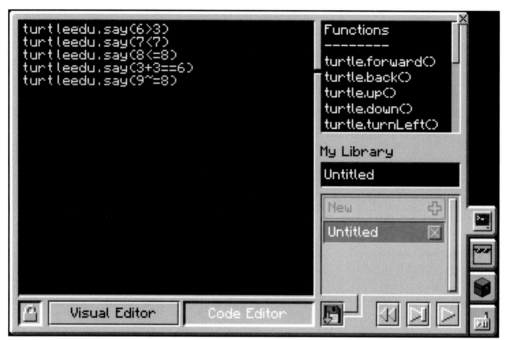

Image 10.7

Did the turtle answer all the questions correctly? You probably already know that yes, it did.

Image 10.8

Exercise 64

Let's write a program that will make the turtle say whether:

- 3 > 6 is true or false;
- 2 < 2 is true or false;
- 11 ≥ 11 is true or false;
- 4 + 4 = 40 is true or false.

Exercise 65
Create the variable x = 8.
Write a program that will check whether x=2.

Exercise 66
Let's write a program together. It will make the turtle count down from 6 to 1 on the variable x, but instead of a number, it will say whether $x <= 3$ in the chat.

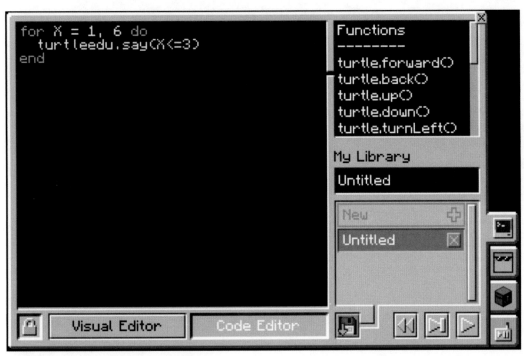

Image 10.9

Image 10.10

Let's add another variable, Y = 4. The program should check whether X is not equal to Y.

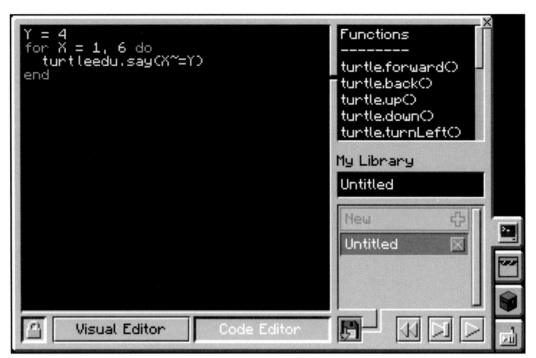

Image 10.11

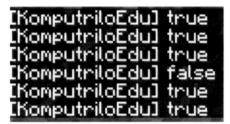

Image 10.12

Exercise 67
Look at the program below and analyze whether the turtle will say true or false for each line.

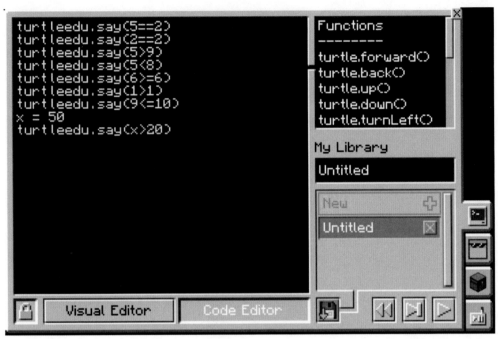

Image 10.13

Exercise 68
Now try to answer some harder questions. Will the turtle say true or false?

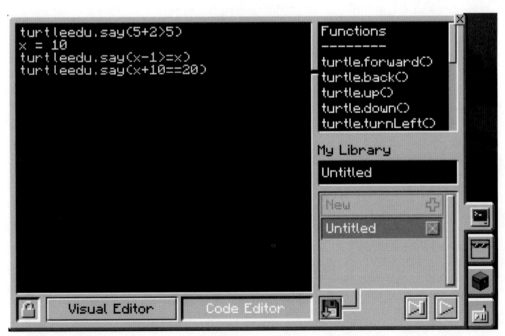

Image 10.14

The if conditional statement

Now that you know how the turtle decides what's true and false, we can go on to learning a new statement, which is if.

Do you know what if means? In programming, it means something dependent on a condition, which you put after the statement itself. It can be any expression from the previous chapter.

What do you say when it's cold? When it's cold, you say "brrr". Let's make the turtle do that.

- If it's cold (true), then the turtle says brr… brr… (end).

Go to the editor and create a variable called cold with the value of true.

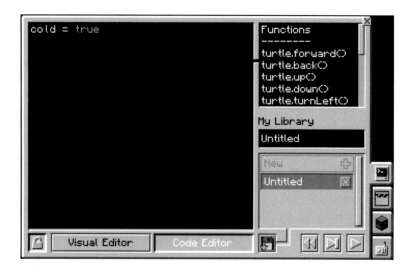

Image 10.15

Now add if. After that, put the condition. Our task is to check whether cold == true.

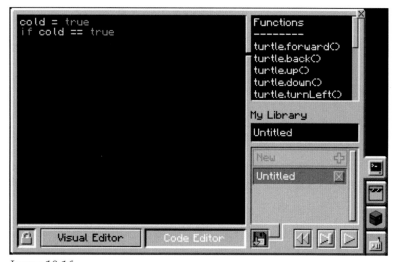

Image 10.16

Now put in then, and put end below it.

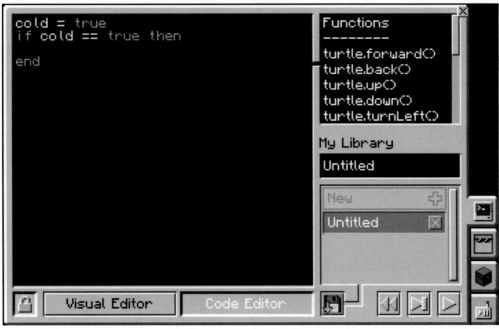

Image 10.17

The if statement will execute the code fragment put between then and end if the condition is true. Now let's tell the turtle to say "brr... brr..." if it's cold.

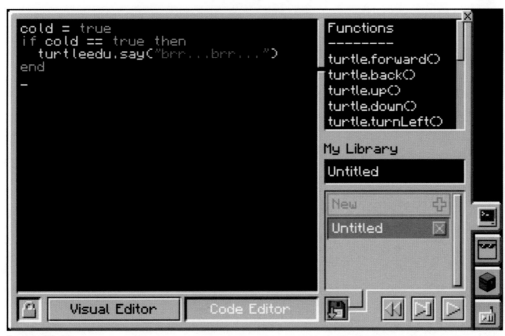

Image 10.18

What will happen if you run the program? The turtle will say „brr… brr…", because cold == true is true.

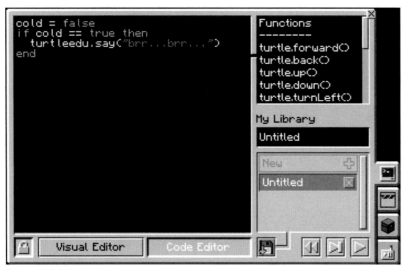

Image 10.19

And what will happen if you change the value of the cold variable to false? Will the turtle say anything?

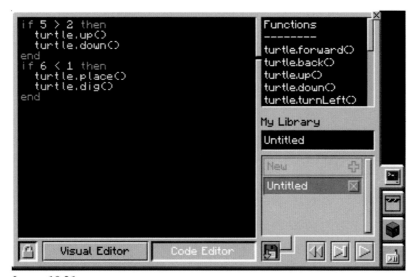

Image 10.20

Of course not because now the condition of cold == true is false. Such the condition is called an unfulfilled condition. In our program, the unfulfilled condition caused the program to skip the turtleedu.say() function.

Exercise 69

Look at the program and say what will the turtle do in this case?

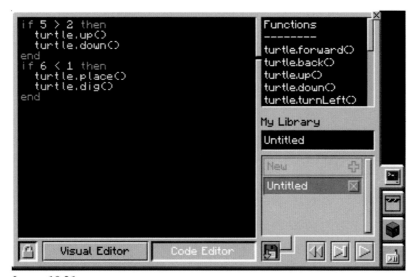

Image 10.21

Exercise 70

Look at the program below and say what should you put into the x variable to make the turtle dance?

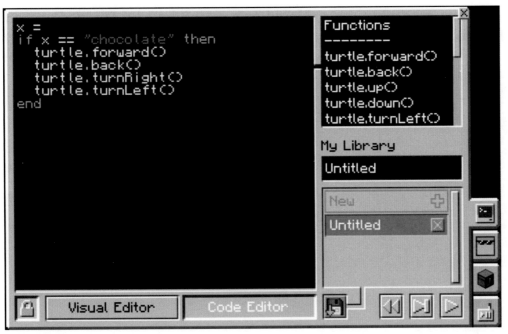

Image 10.22

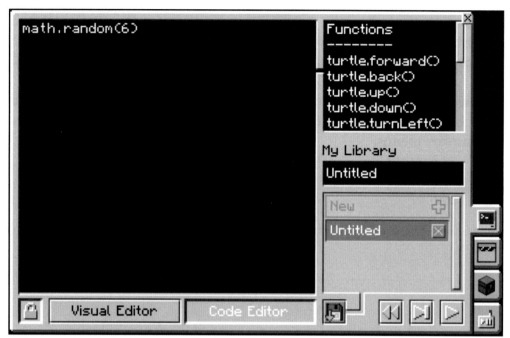

Image 10.26

You can display the selected number in the chat.

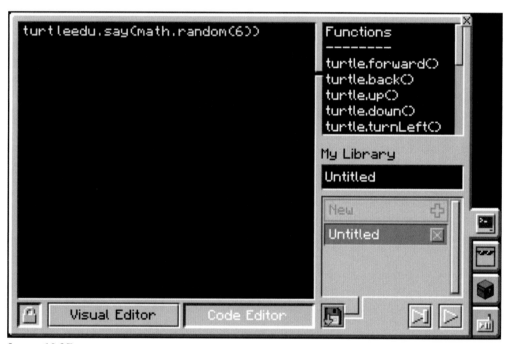

Image 10.27

Or save it in a variable and display the value of a variable.

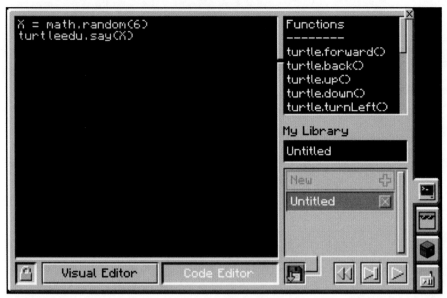

Image 10.28

In the two programs above, the turtle will display the randomly selected number in the chat.

[KomputriloEdu] 3

Image 10.29

Exercise 72
Let's write a program that will make the turtle say a random number between 1 and 10 ten times over.

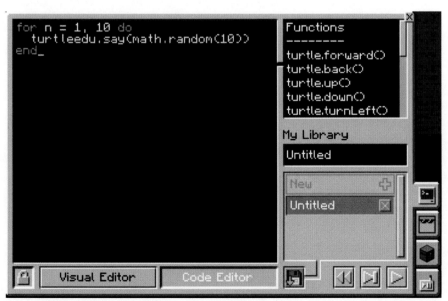

Image 10.30

Exercise 73

Put a few furnaces, chests, and crafting tables in the turtle's inventory.

Write a program that will make the turtle select a random slot between 1 and 3 and then place a block from that slot and go up.

You can run the program several times.

Image 10.31

Exercise 74

Write a program that will make the turtle draw a random number between 1 and 3 and save it into the x variable. It should do something different for each selected number:

- For x=1, the turtle should put a sign on its head.
- For x=2, the turtle should dig one block down and go down.
- For x=3, the turtle should turn around twice.

Exercise 75

Write a program that will make the turtle select a random number between 1 and 10 and save it into a variable called HP. Then:

- If HP<3, the turtle should say "Low HP" and place a brick block in front of it.
- If HP >=3, the turtle should jump.

Exercise 76

Place the turtle on a flat, empty space. Then write a program that will make the turtle draw a number between 1 and 2.

- If the number is equal to 1, the turtle should say "Ahoy captain" and pour water out of a bucket.
- If the number is equal to 2, the turtle should say "I'm hiding" and put a picture in front of itself.

Describe what should be in what slot of the inventory using comments in the code.

Image 10.32

The else statement

The else statement is an extension of the if statement.

To use the else statement, you first to need to use the if statement in the code, and then put else in. It's like that because you first need to do some commands if a condition is met, and else do something different.

To use this instruction, you will put code for if between then and else, and the code that should be done if the condition is not met, between else and end.

Look at the image below and try to figure out which code fragment will be executed: the one below if, or the one below else?

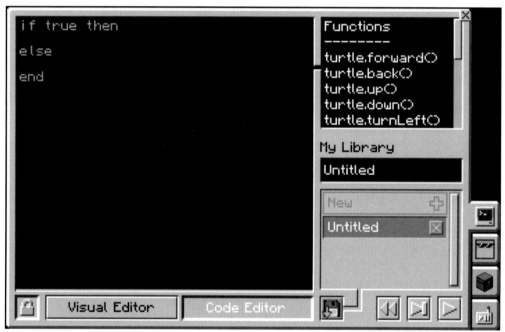

Image 10.33

Of course, it will be just the one under if, because the condition in if is true. So nothing under else is executed.

What if we put in false instead of true? Then the condition in if will be unfulfilled and the code under else will be executed.

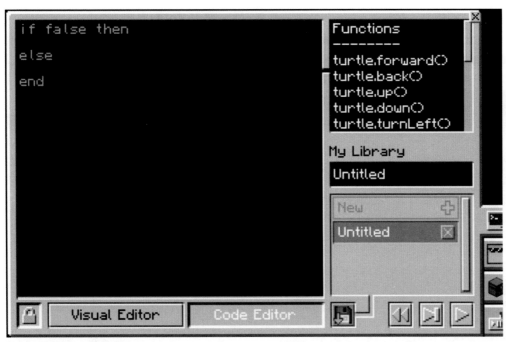

Image 10.34

Exercise 77
Look at the program below and say what is the turtle doing.

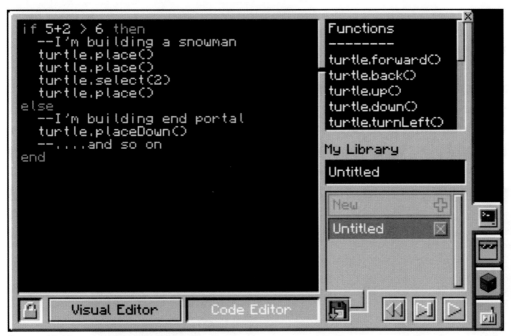

Image 10.35

Exercise 82

Let's write a program that will make the turtle count up from 1 to 10. If it counts above 5, it should build a sponge path under itself and go forward.

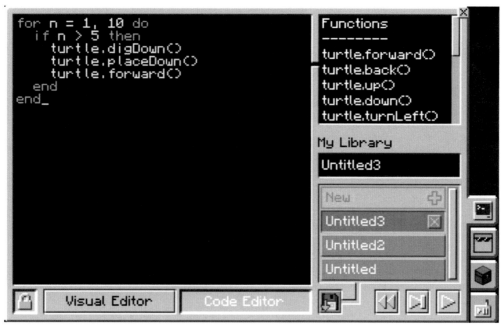

Image 10.39

Let's modify the program above so that the turtle says the loop variable value if the if condition is not met.

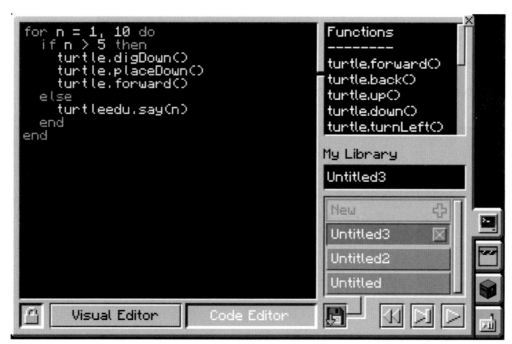

Image 10.40

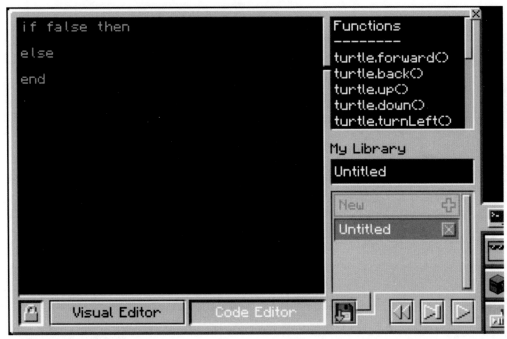

Image 10.34

Exercise 77
Look at the program below and say what is the turtle doing.

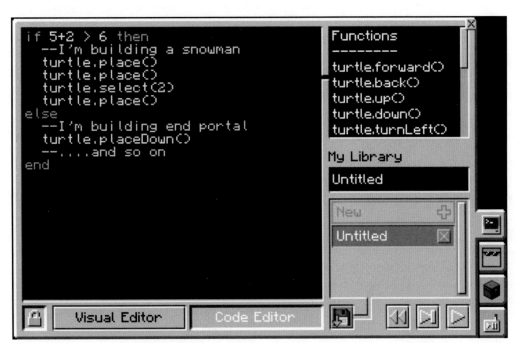

Image 10.35

Exercise 78

Look at the program below and explain why will the turtle turn around instead of placing a block on its head?

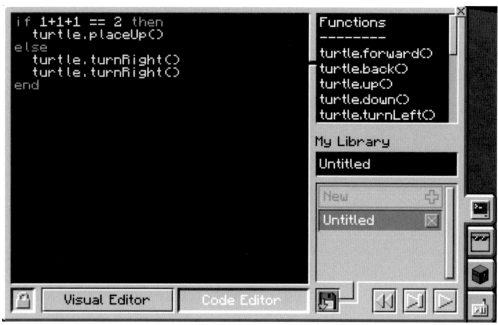

Image 10.36

Exercise 79

Place a Mooshroom egg in the turtle's first inventory, and a cow egg into the second slot.

Write a program that will make the turtle draw a number between 1 and 10, and then:
- If the number is equal or greater than 8, the turtle should place a Mooshroom and say "Something is wrong".
- Else it should place a regular cow.
-

Image 10.37

Stop for a while and think if there's a greater chance for the turtle to place a normal or a mushroom cow?

Of course, the normal one. The turtle will place a regular cow for numbers between 1 and 7, and to place a mooshrom, it has to draw 8, 9, or 10.

Exercise 80

Let's write a program. It should make the turtle draw a number between 1 and 2. If the number selected is 1, then the turtle should say "Heads". Else it should say "Tails".

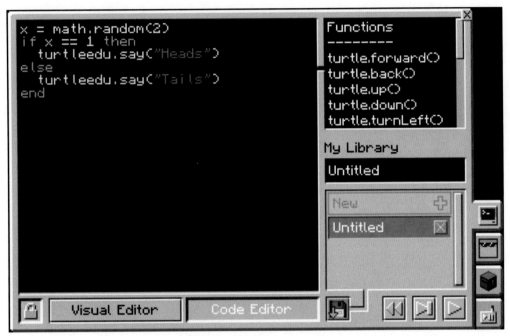

Image 10.38

Which has a greater chance of happening – heads or tails? The chances are equal.

Exercise 81

Write a program that will make the turtle decide randomly whether it will walk a 100 steps ahead, or go up a 100 times.

Exercise 82

Let's write a program that will make the turtle count up from 1 to 10. If it counts above 5, it should build a sponge path under itself and go forward.

Image 10.39

Let's modify the program above so that the turtle says the loop variable value if the if condition is not met.

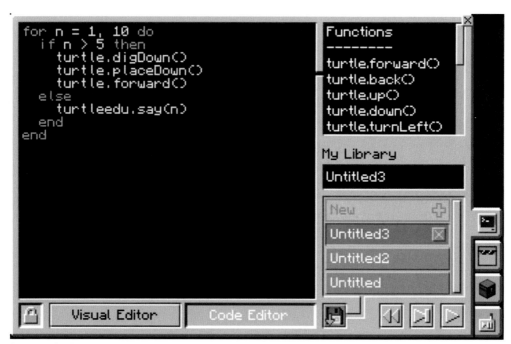

Image 10.40

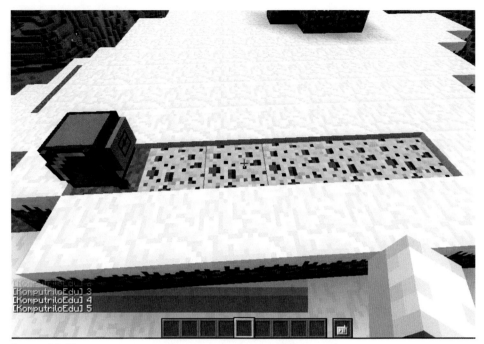

Image 10.41

Exercise 83

Place the turtle three blocks high and write a program that will make it count up from 1 to 20.

If the turtle counts under 15, it should place villagers in front of itself, and else it should place zombies.

Image 10.42

The elseif statement

The elseif is one of the conditional statements. It's a combination of if and else statements and should be understood "else and if that happens, do this". In the code, the elseif instruction is always between if and else (which is optional).

Thanks to if, the program will execute some code when a condition is true. If it's false, the program can go to the elseif instruction (if it's in the code), and execute a different piece of code, if the elseif condition is true.

For example: "If I like the carrots, I will buy more of them, but else if I like watermelons, I will buy them instead of carrots."

So, according to the sentence above, is it enough for watermelons to be tasty so they are bought? No, because first, you have to realize that carrots aren't tasty because the sentence clearly says that the carrots have priority on the shopping list.

See how to program this for the turtle. Instead of buying, the turtle can plant carrots or watermelons. Let's start with building a small farm for it.

Image 10.43

Put carrots in the first slot of the turtle's inventory, and watermelon seeds in the second slot.

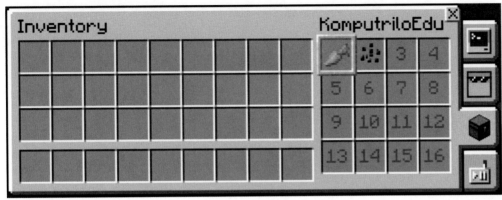

Image 10.44

Create two variables called Carrot and Melon. The Carrot variable stores information whether our turtle likes carrots and the Melon variable contains information whether it likes watermelon.

Let's write a program that will make the turtle solve our dilemma for Carrot = false (it doesn't like carrots) and Melon = true (it likes watermelon).

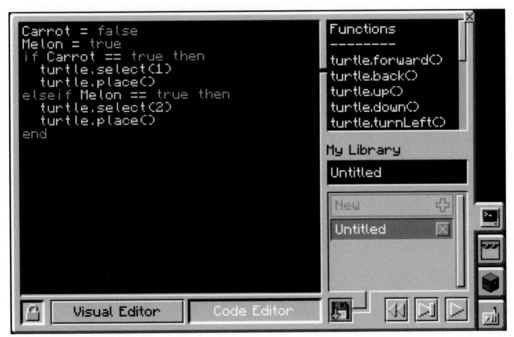

Image 10.45

Will the above program make the turtle plant carrots? No, because the Carrot variable is false.

The program will now go to the elseif condition. Will the turtle plant melons? Yes, because the Melon variable is true.

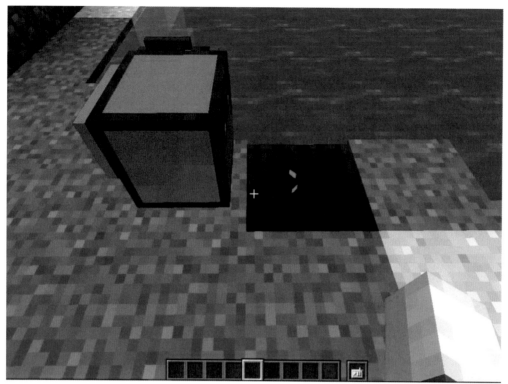

Image 10.46

Exercise 84

Look at the program from the previous example and fill out the table by writing whether the turtle will plant carrots or melons for the given variable values.

Carrot = false Melon = true	
Carrot = true Melon = true	
Carrot = true Melon = false	
Carrot = false Melon = false	

Can you explain why will the turtle only plant carrots if both variables are true?

It's like that because the program will first check if the if condition is true or false. If it turns out to be true, the program will only run the code for the if statement, and then go straight to the code below the end statement, skipping the elseif statement.

Exercise 85.

Look at the programs below and say what will happen:

1.

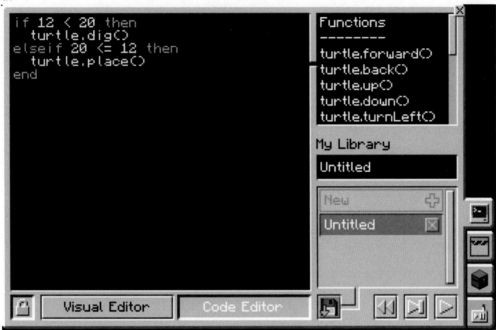

Image 10.47

2.

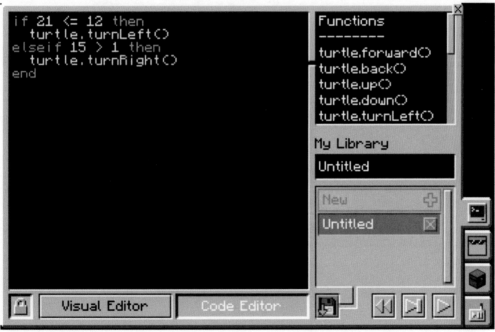

Image 10.48

3.

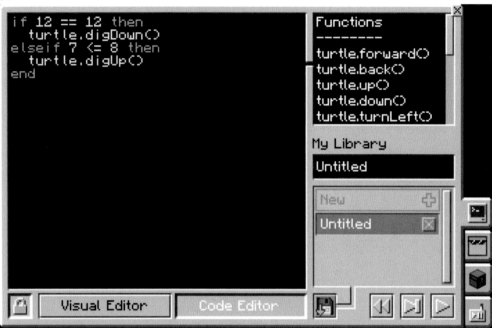

Image 10.49

4.

Image 10.50

Exercise 86

Write a program that will make the turtle draw a number between 1 and 3, save it in the X variable and do something different for each number.

- If X==1, the turtle should say "I am a shepherd" in the chat.
- Else if X==2, the turtle should go two steps up.
- Else the turtle should place a sheep.

Image 10.51

Exercise 87

Place blocks of iron, gold and diamond in the inventory.

Write a program that will make the turtle draw a number between 1 and 10.

Then, if:

- The drawn number is lower or equal to 3, it should place a block of iron.
- If that condition is not met, but the number is lower than 6, the turtle should place a block of gold.
- Else it should place a block of diamond.

Exercise 88

Place the turtle on the ground and put five anvils in its inventory.
Write a program that will make the turtle count in a for loop for n 1 to 12.

- If n < 5, the turtle should say the n value in the chat.
- Else if n <10 the turtle should go one block up and place an anvil.
- Else, it should go two blocks down and dig one block in front of itself.

Image 10.52

Exercise 89

Say what three instructions can help you command the code through conditions.

Logic operands

Logic operands can be used in conditions.
In the Lua language, we have 3 operands – **and, or, and not.**

The and logic operand.

The and operator can combine conditions, just like the word "and" does in spoken language.
Example: If I don't have a cat and I'm not allergic, I can adopt a puppy.
Look at the table showing all possible situations for this condition:

true and true	true	true and true -> true
true and false	false	true and false -> false
false and true	false	false and true -> false
false and false	false	false and false -> false

Exercise 90

Look at the programs below and say whether the turtle will jump.

1.

Image 10.53

2.

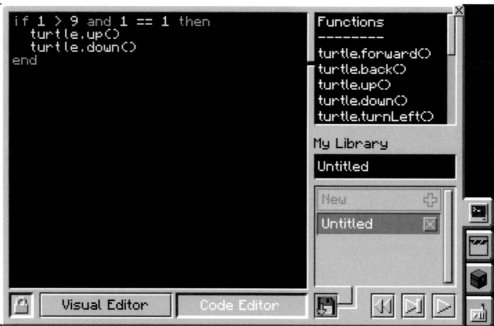

Image 10.54

3.

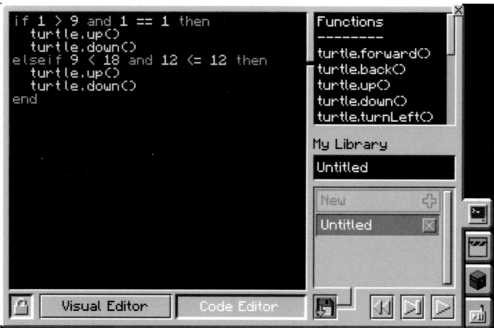

Image 10.55

The or logic operand

The or operand is used to combine conditions, same as the word "or" in spoken language.

Example: If I have money or win a competition, I can buy a new bike.

Here's a table showing all possible situations for this condition:

true or true	true	true or true -> true
true or false	true	true or false -> true
false or true	true	false or true -> true
false or false	false	false or false -> false

Exercise 91

Look at the programs below and say whether the turtle will jump.

1.

Image 10.56

2.

```
if 5 == 3 or 15 <= 14 then
   turtle.up()
   turtle.down()
end
```

Functions
----

turtle.forward()
turtle.back()
turtle.up()
turtle.down()
turtle.turnLeft()

My Library

Untitled

New

Untitled

Visual Editor   Code Editor

Image 10.57

3.

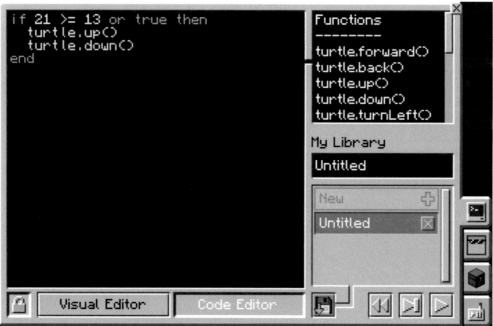

```
if 21 >= 13 or true then
   turtle.up()
   turtle.down()
end
```

Functions
----

turtle.forward()
turtle.back()
turtle.up()
turtle.down()
turtle.turnLeft()

My Library

Untitled

New

Untitled

Visual Editor   Code Editor

Image 10.58

The not logic operand

The not operand can be used to change the value of the condition.

Let's say it's raining and create two conditions, one using the not operand, and the other without it.

If it's raining, I will play board games.

If it's not raining, I will play soccer.

Here's a table showing all possible situations for this condition:

not true	false	Not true, so false
not false	true	Not false, so true

Keep in mind that the not operand can only be used with values that can be interpreted as true or false. It can be the "5>2" condition, for example, but writing "not 5>2" will cause a program error. It's because the program will combine the not operand with the number 5, and not the whole condition.

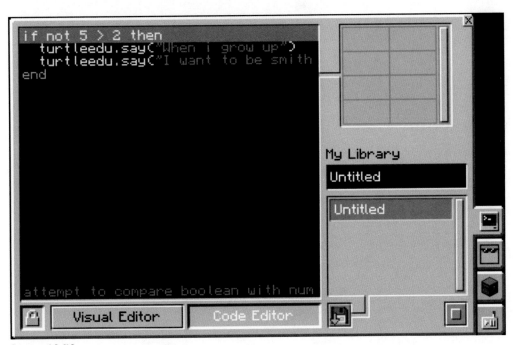

Image 10.59

To get rid of the mistake, you need to tell the program that the 5>2 expression needs to be considered separately. To do it, you need to lock it in round brackets.

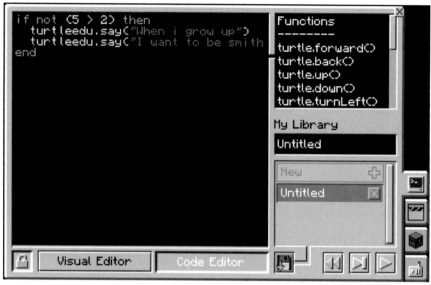

Image 10.60

Will the turtle display a text after the program has been edited properly? The expression in the brackets is true, but the not logic operand changes it to false. So the turtle will not say anything.

Exercise 92

Look at the programs below and try to say whether the turtle will place and destroy a block.

1.

Image 10.61

2.

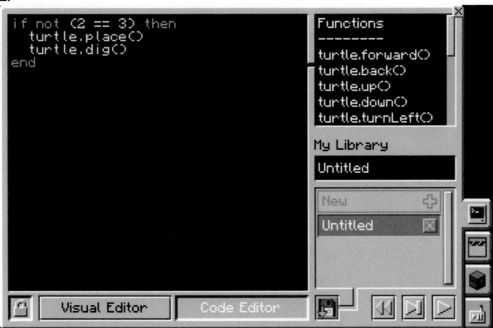

```
if not (2 == 3) then
   turtle.place()
   turtle.dig()
end
```

Functions
----
turtle.forward()
turtle.back()
turtle.up()
turtle.down()
turtle.turnLeft()

My Library

Untitled

New
Untitled

Visual Editor   Code Editor

Image 10.62

3.

```
if not (11 >= 17) then
   turtle.place()
   turtle.dig()
end
```

Functions
----
turtle.forward()
turtle.back()
turtle.up()
turtle.down()
turtle.turnLeft()

My Library

Untitled

New
Untitled

Visual Editor   Code Editor

Image 10.63

Exercise 93

Let's write a program that will make the turtle count up for n from 1 to 9.
- If n <3 or n>7, the turtle should turn around.
- Else if n==3 or n==6, the turtle should go one block up.
- Else if n is no smaller than 5, the turtle should place a block of cobblestone below itself.

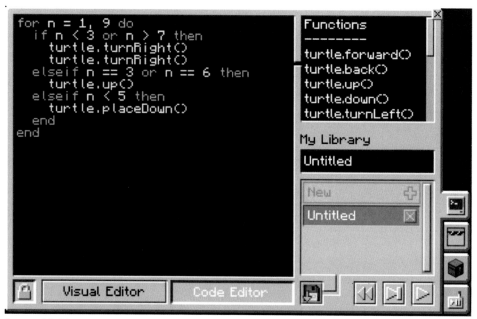

Image 10.64

Image 10.65

Exercise 94

Looking at the previous exercise, assign numbers for which the turtle will execute an action to each action in the table below. You can do this task while observing the turtle.

Turn around	
Go one block up	
Place a block below itself	
Do nothing	

Chapter 11: Redstone

In Minecraft, you can build machines using redstone dust. It can be active or inactive. If it's active and glowing, it will activate all connected devices.

Pour some redstone dust and connect it to a lamp and a lever as shown in the image below.

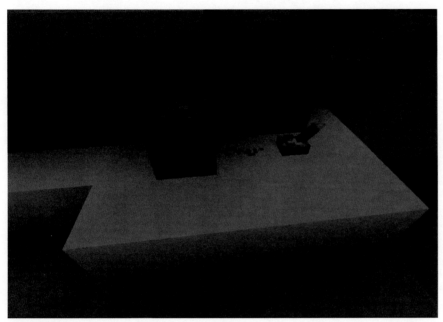

Image 11.1

Switching the lever will cause the redstone dust to activate and the lamp to turn on.

Image 11.2

Exercise 95

Place a lamp and pour some redstone in front of it. Put turtle one block away from the redstone dust, as shown in the image below.

Image 11.3

Put a redstone torch into the turtle's inventory.

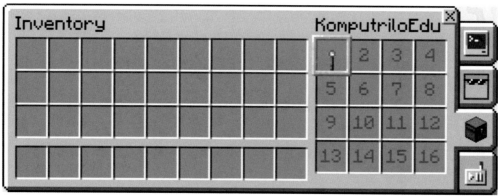

Image 11.4

Write a program that will make the turtle place and collect the redstone church alternately, 50 times.

The turtleedu.checkRedstone() function.

Redstone can be active or not.

The turtleedu.checkRedstone() function can be used to check whether redstone is active. If it is, the turtle will return true. If we deactivate the redstone, it will return false.

Let's check how it works.

Exercise 96

Pour some redstone in front of the turtle and connect it to a lever as in the image below.

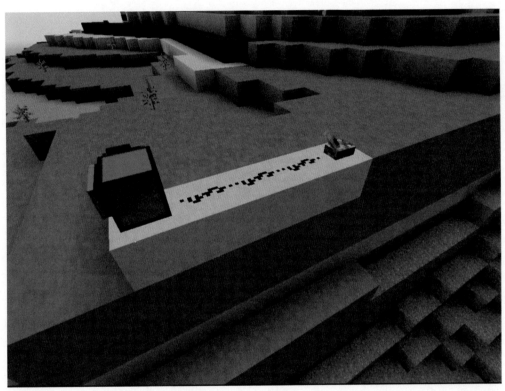

Image 11.5

Let's write a program that will make the turtle say the state of the redstone dust in the chat.

```
turtleedu.say(turtleedu.checkRedstone())
```

Image 11.6

If the redstone dust is inactive, the function returns false. Then the value is displayed in the chat using turtleedu.say().

Image 11.7

If it's active, the function will return true.

Image 11.8

As you can see, the function returns logic values, so it can be used in programs with conditional statements.

Exercise 97
Put a lava bucket in the turtle's active inventory slot.
Write a program that will make the turtle pour lava on its head if it detects active redstone in front of itself. Else it should take a step forward.

Image 11.9

Exercise 98
Write a program that will make the turtle dig a hole 10 blocks deep after detecting active redstone in front of itself. Else, it should dig a hole 20 blocks deep.

The turtleedu.checkRedstoneUp() function

The turtleedu.checkRedstoneUp() checks whether there's active redstone dust above the turtle. If yes, it returns true.

Exercise 99
Let's write a program that will check whether redstone dust above the turtle is active.

```
turtleedu.say(turtleedu.checkRedstoneUp())
```
Image 11.10

Let's place a block on the turtle's head and pour some redstone dust on it, then connect it to a lever. If you don't activate the redstone dust, the turtle will say false.

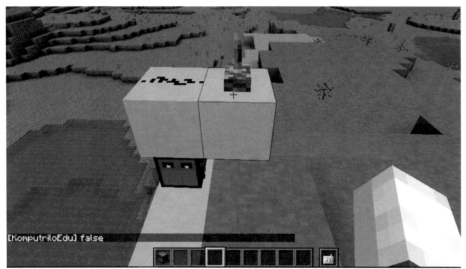
Image 11.11

Else, if the dust is active, the turtle should say true.

Image 11.12

Exercise 100 (WOW!)
Write a program that will make the turtle collect the block above itself after detecting active redstone dust above.

The turtleedu.checkRedstoneDown() function

As you can see by the name, you can expect that this function will check whether there's active redstone dust below the turtle. But here's a surprise.

Using turtleedu.checkRedstoneDown(), despite it having "Down" in the name, you can check whether there's active redstone dust behind the turtle.

Exercise 101
Let's write a program that will make the turtle say whether there's active redstone dust behind it, but activate it under the turtle.

```
turtleedu.say(turtleedu.checkRedstoneDown())
```
Image 11.13

The function will not return true if the activated redstone dust is below the turtle.

Image 11.14

Using this function, you can check whether there's active redstone behind the turtle. Let's change our construction so that the redstone dust is behind the turtle.

Image 11.15

Exercise 102

Write a program that will make the turtle display a random number between 1 and 100 after detecting active redstone behind itself.

Image 11.16

Exercise 103

Let's write a program that will make the turtle save the state of redstone below it, above it, and behind it in the F, U, and Z variables. Then, if any of the variables is true, the turtle should say "I feel power". Else, it should say "No electricity".

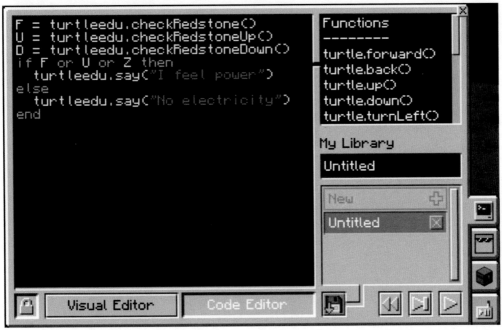

Image 11.17

Exercise 104

Write a program that will start with the variable x =0, and then:
- If there's active redstone in front of the turtle, x should increase by 1.
- If there's active redstone above the turtle, x should increase by 2.
- If there's active redstone behind the turtle, x should increase by 4.
- At the end, the turtle should say the x value.

What number will the turtle display if we activate redstone dust above and behind it?

The turtleedu.setRedstone() function

The turtle can activate or deactivate redstone dust in front of itself using the turtleedu.setRedstone() function.

To change the state of redstone dust, you can use the following functions:
- In front of the turtle – turtleedu.setRedstone()
- Above the turtle – turtleedu.setRedstoneUp()
- Behind the turtle – turtleedu.setRedstoneDown()

Exercise 105
Place six relays in front of the turtle. Keep in mind, they need to be placed so that the arrow points from the turtle to the other relay, as in the image below.

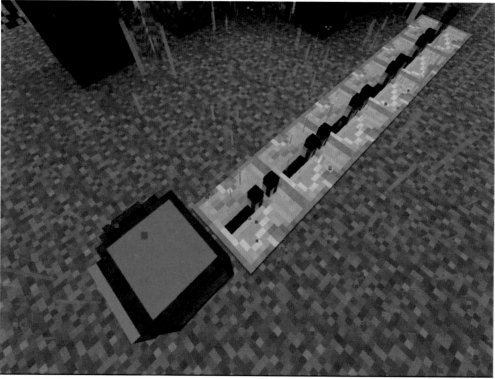

Image 11.18

To activate the first relay, you need to use a function that can change the state of the redstone in front of the turtle. The argument between the brackets can be true or false, which will set the value of the redstone.
- True - activate the redstone dust,
- False – deactivate the redstone dust.

Let's write a program that will make the turtle activate the relays.

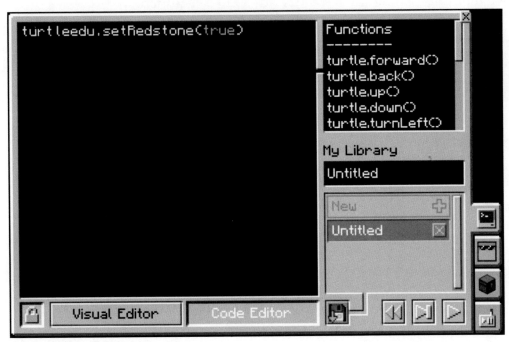

Image 11.19

The relays will activate one after another and remain turned on.

Image 11.20

The relays will remain activated until you remove the turtle.

You can also set the state of the redstone dust to inactive using a different program. To do that, we'll use the same function, but with a false argument.

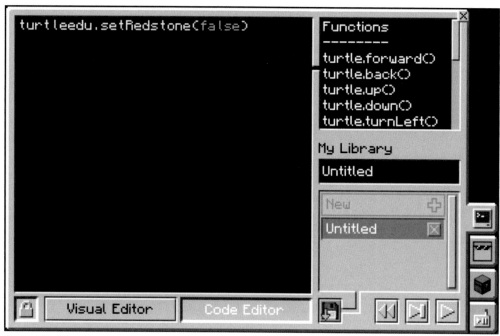

Image 11.21

Exercise 106

Add at least four more relays. Write a program that will make the turtle activate and deactivate the redstone dust in front of itself.

Image 11.22

Exercise 107
Place a dispenser in front of the turtle and fill it with diamonds.

Image 11.23

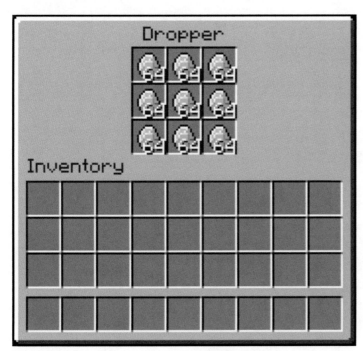

Image 11.24

Write a program that will make the turtle activate and deactivate the dispenser when it detects active redstone behind itself. Keep in mind that a block of redstone acts like active redstone dust.

Image 11.25

Exercise 108
Write a program that will make the turtle place two note blocks in front of itself, and then activate redstone in front of itself.

Image 11.26

Exercise 109

Put TNT in the first slot of the turtle's inventory, and then a block of stone in the second one. Put the turtle on the ground.

Write a program that will make the turtle place a block of TNT and activate it.

Then the turtle should dig itself 2 blocks deep and put a block of stone over itself.

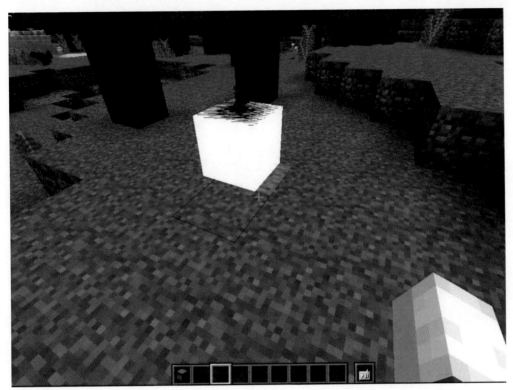

Image 11.27

Exercise 110
Place a dispenser pointing up in front of the turtle and fill it with enchanted bottles.

Exercise 11.28

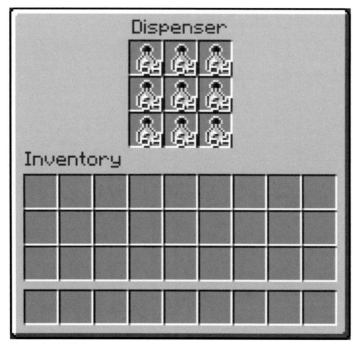

Exercise 11.29

Write a program that will make the turtle activate and deactivate the dispenser 64 times.

Image 11.30

Exercise 111

Place pistons in front, above, and behind the turtle, pointing up.

Image 11.31

Write a program that will make the turtle choose x between 1 and 3 randomly fifty times, and:

- If X = 1, the turtle activates and deactivates the piston in front of itself.
- If X = 2, the turtle activates and deactivates the piston above of itself.
- If X = 3, the turtle activates and deactivates the piston behind itself.

The piston extends when there's active redstone next to it. That's why you need to use three activating redstone functions.

Chapter 12: The while loop

You can repeat code fragments in different ways than with the for loop. That's what you can use the while loop for. It will run a code fragment as long as the condition in it is true.

Exercise 112
Let's place some redstone and a redstone torch in front of the turtle.

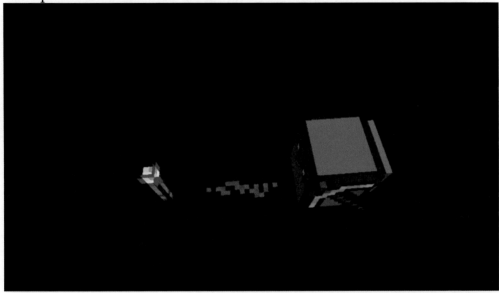

Image 12.1

Let's write a program that will make the turtle jump as long as it detects active redstone in front of itself.

Image 12.2

After running the program, the turtle will jump as long as the redstone dust is activated. So the while loop runs a code fragment between the do and end statements for as long as the turtleedu.checkRedstone() returns true.

After deactivating the redstone dust, the turtleedu.checkRedstone() will return false, which will cause the loop to stop. The program will then move to the first line of code following the end instruction. In this case, it means the end of the program.

Exercise 113
Put sixty four blocks of emerald into the turtle's inventory.
Build a redstone block tower at least ten blocks tall behind the turtle.
Place the turtle on the ground, facing away from the tower.

Exercise 12.3

Write a program that will make the turtle place a block of emerald in front of itself and go up as long as it detects active redstone behind itself. Keep in mind that the redstone block acts like active redstone dust.

Image 12.4

Exercise 114

Let's write a program that will make the turtle assign the value 0 to the number X. Then it should randomly draw a new value for X between 1 and 20 and display it as long as X is below 18.

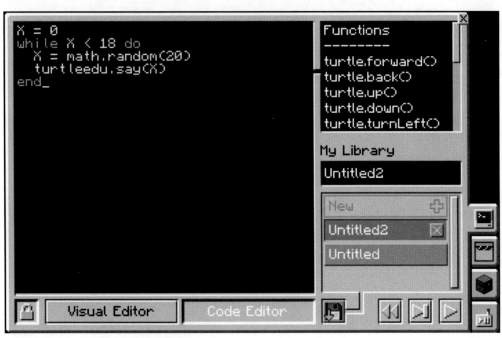

Image 12.5

Image 12.6

Exercise 115
Place lamps in front of and behind the turtle, and a block of redstone on the turtle.

Image 12.7

Write a program that will make the turtle turn the lamps on and off alternately as long as it detects a source of active redstone above itself, it being the redstone block.

Infinite programs

Exercise 116

Let's write a program that will make the turtle display the string "I'm alive", as long as 5>2.

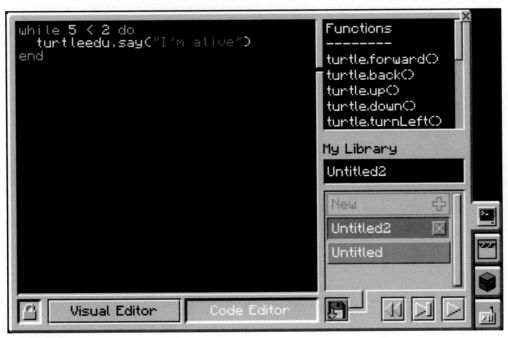

Image 12.8

Think about it: for how long will the turtle write that text in the chat?

It'll be doing it infinitely because the 5>2 condition is always true.

Using the while loop, you can write programs that will work until they're manually stopped. You just need to put something that's always true as a condition. The simplest way is to use the true value because then the program will not have to calculate the condition value every time.

Exercise 117
Place an iron door in front of the turtle.

Image 12.9

Let's write a program that will make the turtle open and close and close the door infinitely.

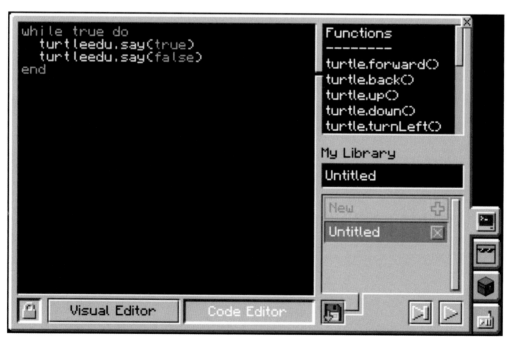

Image 12.10

Exercise 118

Write a program that will make the turtle infinitely draw a random number between 1 and 2, save it into the x variable, and then do a different thing depending on the value.

- If X=1, the turtle should place and dig up a watermelon.
- If X=2, the turtle should say "Enjoy your meal".

Have you noticed what happens with the watermelon, when the turtle digs it up? Watermelon slices end up in the inventory instead of a watermelon block.

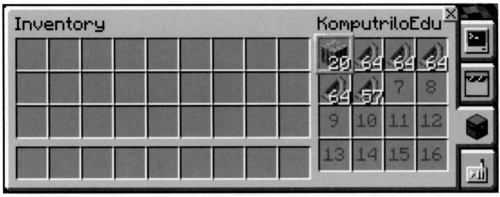

Image 12.11

Exercise 119
Build an empty hoop 5x5 using light blue glass blocks.

Image 12.12

Write a program that will make the turtle infinitely walk around the hoop.

Chapter 13: Detecting blocks

The turtle.detect() function

Place a piston one block away from the turtle, and then put a lever next to it.

Image 13.1

Now you will learn a function that will check whether there's a block in front of the turtle.

The function is called turtle.detect(). It works like this: if there's a block in front of the turtle, it returns true, and if not, it returns false. So it simply answers the question – is there a block in front of the turtle?

Exercise 120
Let's write a program that will make the turtle infinitely say whether there's a block in front of it. Then check how the turtle.detect() function works by extending and retracting the piston.

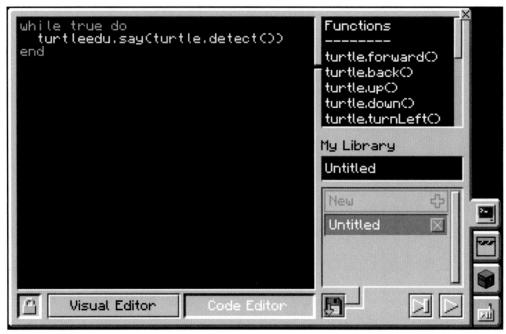

Image 13.2

What will the turtle say when the piston is retracted? False, of course. And when it's extended? Then it'll say true because there's a piston piece in front of it.

Image 13.3

Exercise 121
Write a program that will make the turtle walk forward infinitely, and destroy a block in front of itself if it detects one.

Exercise 122
Place the turtle in the air, eight blocks away from a tree, and fill its active slot with yellow wool blocks.

Image 13.4

Write a program that will make the turtle place a block of wool under front of itself and go forward as long as there are no blocks in front of it.

Image 13.5

Exercise 128

Write a program that will make the turtle infinitely check whether there's a block in front of it. If there is, the turtle should say "I don't see!".

Exercise 124

Cobblestone is created when water meets flowing lava. Using this, we can create a cobblestone generator.

Build a simple cobblestone generator. To do it, create ditch ten blocks long. Pour water on one end, and lava on the other. Place the turtle as in the picture below.

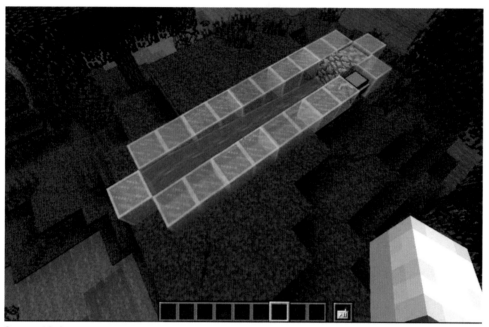

Image 13.6

Write a program that will make the turtle infinitely check whether there's a block in front of it. If there is, it should dig it and display "+1 Cobblestone" in the chat.

Image 13.7

Remaining turtle.detect() functions

Tho check whether there's a block next to the turtle, you can also use the following functions:

- turtle.detectDown() - the turtle will check whether there's a block under it;
- turtle.detectUp() - the turtle will check whether there's a block above it.

Exercise 125

Let's write a program that will make the turtle collect a block and put it on its head if it detects a block below itself.

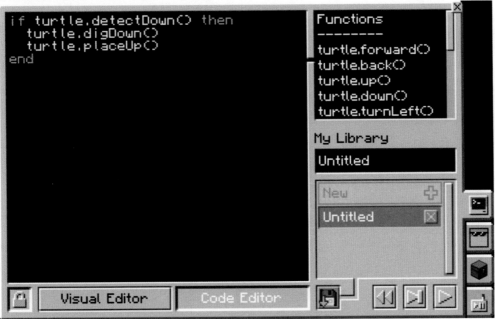

Image 13.8

Image 13.9

Exercise 126

Write a program in which the turtle detects whether there's a block above it and if there is, it should go around it and stand on it.

Exercise 127

Write a program that will make the turtle:
- if it detects a block in front of itself, it should destroy it, then place and activate TNT;
- Else if it detects a block under itself, it should dig down;
- Else if it detects a block above itself, it should display a random number between 1 and 80.

Exercise 128

Solve the riddle concerning the previous task:
If the turtle displayed the number 42 in the chat, has it detected a block in front of under itself?

The turtleedu.inspect() function

Using the turtleedu.inspect() function, you can check what specific block is in front of the turtle. The function returns the block name.

Minecraft has been created in English, and as such, all the names will be in English.

Exercise 129

Let's write a program that will make the turtle say what block is in front of it.

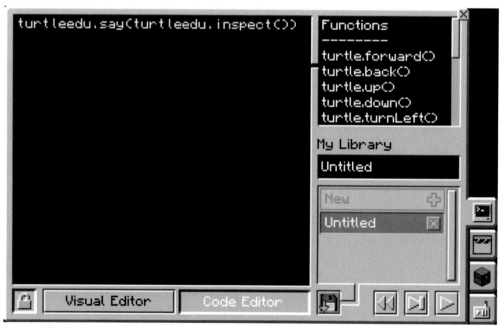

Image 13.10

Now let's put a block of red wool in front of it and check what will it say.

Image 13.11

The programmers who created Minecraft added "minecraft:" to every block name.
That's why the turtle will say "minecraft:wool" after detecting the wool.

[KomputriloEdu] minecraft:wool

Image 13.12

Exercise 130

Put a block of coal in the turtle's inventory and place a furnace in front of it.
Create a variable called furnace, which will store a string "minecraft:furnace". Then, the turtle should check whether the block in front of it is called the same as the value in the furnace variable. If it is, it should place the block of coal next to it.

Image 13.13

Exercise 131

Write a program that will make the turtle display "eat" in the chat as long as it doesn't detect a block of iron in front of itself ("minecraft:iron_block"). After exiting the loop, the turtle should display "Healthy iron".

Exercise 132

Write a program that will make the turtle spin until it detects a bed in front of itself
(minecraft:bed).

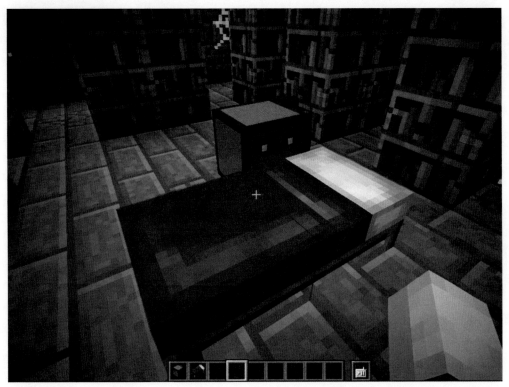

Image 13.14

The other turtleedu.inspect() functions

Aside from the presented turtleedu.inspect(), you can also use two similar functions.
They make it possible to check the objects above and under the turtle.

- turtleedu.inspectUp() - checks what block is above the turtle.
- turtleedu.inspectDown() - checks what block is under the turtle.

Exercise 133

Let's write a program that will make the turtle dig down as long as it doesn't detect bedrock. Bedrock's name is "minecraft:bedrock".

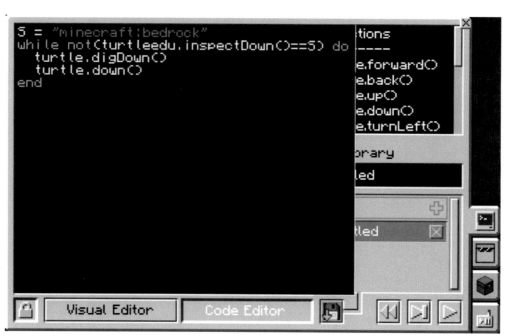

Image 13.15

Exercise 134

Write a program that will make the turtle save the name of the block under itself into the variable down, and the name of the block above itself into the variable up.
Then the turtle should check if the names are the same and if yes, it should display "same blocks" in the chat.

Image 13.16

Exercise 135

Build a path ten blocks long for the turtle, using various blocks from the Building Blocks tab.

Image 13.17

Write a program that will make the turtle say ten times what block is under it and take a step forward.

Image 13.18

Chapter 14: Counting items

The turtle.getItemCount() function

Our turtle can count the amount of items in its active slot. The function used for it is turtle.getItemCount(). It returns the number of items counted by the turtle.

Exercise 136

Put twelve sticks into the turtle's inventory.

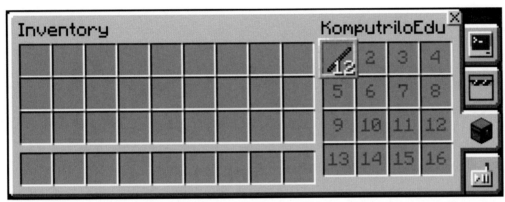

Image 14.1

Let's write a program that will make the turtle say how many items are in its active slot.

Image 14.2

Run the program and check what will the turtle say.

[KomputriloEdu] 12

Image 14.3

The turtle isn't wrong. What will happen if you take half of the sticks? The turtle will say 6, of course.

[KomputriloEdu] 6

Image 14.4

Exercise 137
Put at least one carrot in the turtle's active slot.
Write a program that will make the turtle display a random number between 1 and the number of blocks in its active slot.

Exercise 138
Place the turtle in front of a wall.

Image 14.5

Write a program that will make the turtle dig straight forward as long as it has less than ten blocks in its first slot. After finishing the loop, it should say "finished".

Exercise 139

Place the turtle one block into the air and put eight blocks of sand into its inventory. Write a program that will make the turtle build a sand wall for as long as it has more than zero blocks of sand in its active slot.

Image 14.6

Exercise 140

Let's write a program that will make the turtle save the amount of items in the first slot into X, and the amount of items in the second slot into Y. Then it should display the sum of those two numbers in the chat.

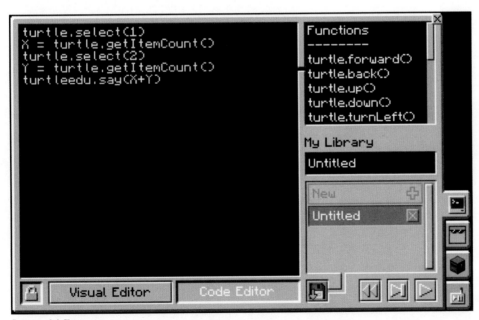

Image 14.7

Chapter 15: The turtle with a watch

The os.sleep() function

Using the code editor, we can use more functions than in the visual editor. One of those functions is os.sleep(), which allows us to run the program for a specific time in seconds.

Exercise 141

Let's write a program that will make the turtle jump after precisely 5 seconds since launching the program.

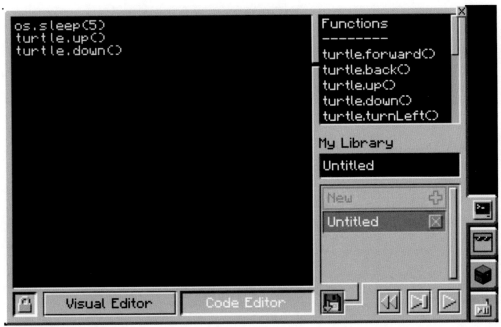

Image 15.1

Exercise 142

Write a program that will make the turtle count from 1 to 10, with each number every second.

Exercise 143

Write a program that will make the turtle display "Horse for sale" in the chat every ten seconds.

Exercise 144

Place a lamp in front of the turtle.

Write a program that will make the turtle turn the lamp on and off every second.

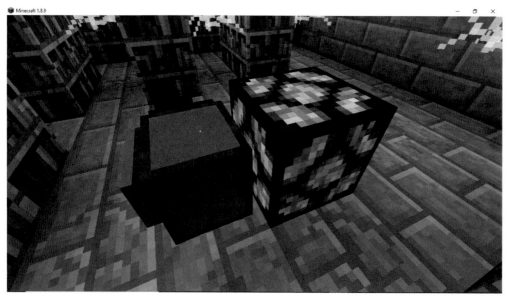

Image 15.2

Exercise 145

Place a few blocks of TNT in the turtle's active inventory.

Write a program that will make the turtle place and detonate a block of TNT after as many seconds as the number of items it has in its active slot.

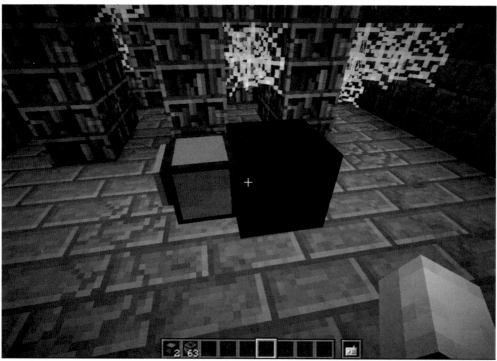

Image 15.3

Chapter 16: What item is that?

The turtleedu.getItemName() function

Using the turtleedu.getItemName() function you can check what item the turtle has in its active slot. The function will return the item name into the program. In the case of blocks, those names will be just like the ones you saw when learning the turtle.inspect() function.

Exercise 146

Place a torch in the turtle's active slot.

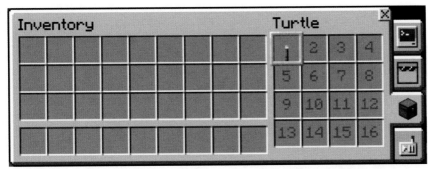

Image 16.1

Let's write a program that will make the turtle display the torch name returned by the turtleedu.getItemName() function in the chat.

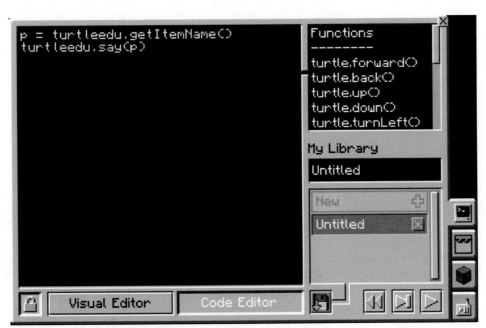

Image 16.2

[KomputriloEdu] minecraft:torch

Image 16.3

Exercise 147

Fill the turtle's inventory with various items from the tools tab.

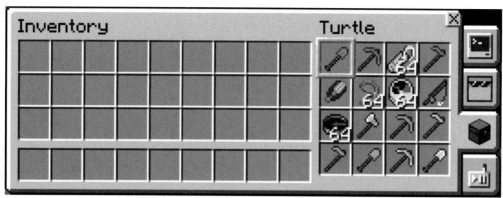

Image 16.4

Now write a program that will make the turtle say what's in each one of the slots.

```
[KomputriloEdu] minecraft:name_tag
[KomputriloEdu] minecraft:stone_hoe
[KomputriloEdu] minecraft:shears
[KomputriloEdu] minecraft:lead
[KomputriloEdu] minecraft:clock
[KomputriloEdu] minecraft:fishing_rod
[KomputriloEdu] minecraft:compass
[KomputriloEdu] minecraft:iron_axe
[KomputriloEdu] minecraft:diamond_pickaxe
[KomputriloEdu] minecraft:golden_hoe
```

Image 16.5

Exercise 148

Put a diamond sword in any one of the turtle's inventory slots.

Write a program that will make the turtle select a random slot until it finds the one containing the diamond sword („minecraft:diamond_sword").

At the end, after exiting the loop, it should say "I'm going to fight".

Exercise 149

Place a jukebox in front of the turtle, and place a jukebox and a few random items in its inventory.

Write a program that will make the turtle search its inventory searching for the block that's the same as the one in front of it. If it finds such a block, it should say "I have it in my inventory" in the chat.

Image 16.6

Exercise 150

Place several blocks of ice in the turtle's inventory.

Let's write a program that will make the turtle infinitely check whether it has a block of ice in its inventory slot ("minecraft:ice"). If it does, it should build a path out of ice under itself until it runs out of ice blocks.

When it runs out of ice blocks, give it some new ones. The turtle will continue to build the path.

Keep in mind, that there are three "ends" in the program. That's because both while and if always have to be closed by an end statement.

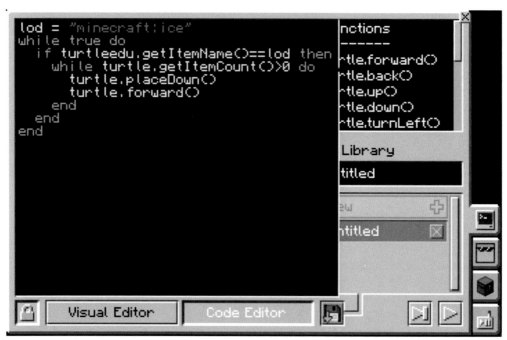

Image 16.7

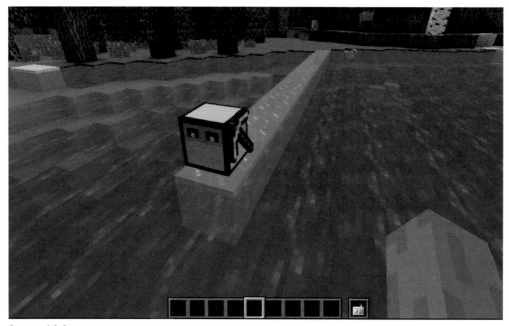

Image 16.8

Chapter 17: The Porter Turtle

The turtle.transferTo() function

Another function that can only be used in the code editor, is the turtle.transferTo() function. It allows the turtle to transfer items from the active slot to a different one.

Exercise 151

Let's put a clock in the first slot of the turtle's inventory.

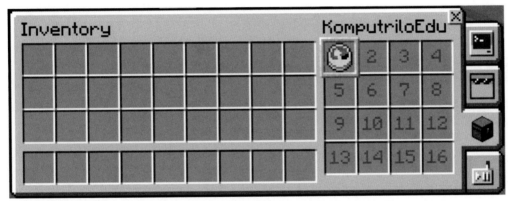

Image 17.1

Now let's write a program that will make the turtle transfer the clock into the last slot.

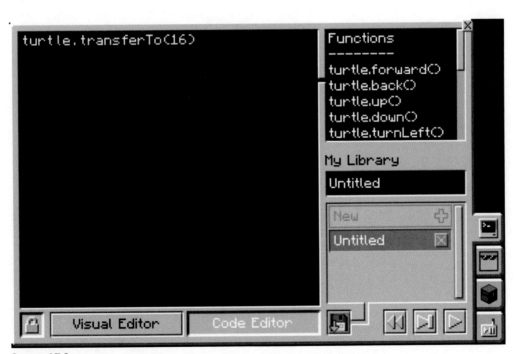

Image 17.2

After running the program, the clock has been transferred from the first slot to the last one.

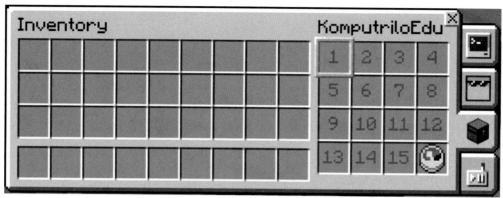

Image 17.3

Exercise 152
Put a minecart in the first slot of the turtle's inventory.
Write a program that will make the turtle infinitely draw a random number between 1 and 16 an then save it into X.
Then it should transfer the item into the randomly selected slot and change the active slot to the randomly selected one.

Exercise 153
Put a gold ingot in any turtle inventory slot except the first one.
Write a program that will make the turtle search slots numbered 2 to 16. If it finds an ingot in the slot ("minecraft:gold_ingot"), it should transfer it to the first slot.

Exercise 154

Let's write a program that will make the turtle do the following if it detects in its first slot:

- A carrot („minecraft:carrot") - transfer it to the fourteenth slot;
- An apple („minecraft:apple") - transfer it to the fifteenth slot;
- A potato („minecraft:potato") - transfer it to the sixteenth slot.

Let's use variables named C, A, and P.

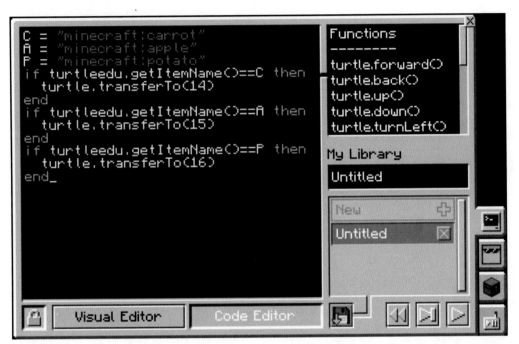

Image 17.4

During the program execution, put, in this order, a few carrots, apples, and potatoes in the turtle's first slot. The turtle will sort them for us until it fills the slots numbered 14, 15, and 16.

The turtle.drop() function

The turtle can put items in chests using the turtle.drop() function. Using this function when there's empty space in front of the turtle will make it throw the item on the ground.

Exercise 155

Put a compass in the turtle's inventory.

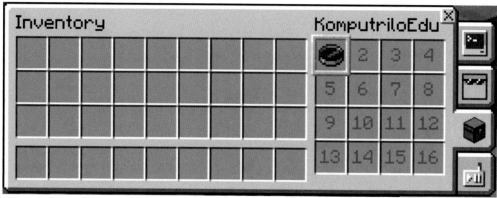

Image 17.5

Place a chest in front of the turtle.

Image 17.6

Now let's write a program that will make the turtle hide the compass in the chest.

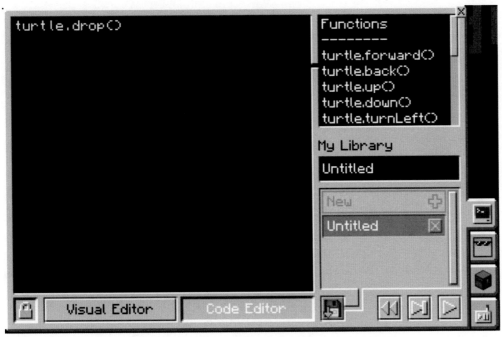

Image 17.7

After the program is executed, the compass is in the chest.

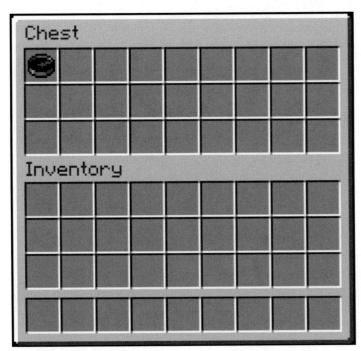

Image 17.8

Exercise 156
Write a program that will make the turtle infinitely check whether there's an item in its' active slot. If it detects one, it should throw it away.

Exercise 157
Place a chest in front of the turtle.

Write a program that will make the turtle dig down ten blocks deep, and then return to the chest and drop the items from its' first slot into it.

Image 17.9

Exercise 158

Place a chest behind the turtle and place ten blocks of cobweb into the turtle's inventory.

Write a program that will make the turtle build a column of three blocks of cobweb behind itself, and put the rest in the chest.

Image 17.10

The turtle.suck() function

The turtle can also take items out of chests. For that, you'll use the turtle.suck() function.

Exercise 159

Put a fishing rod in a chest.

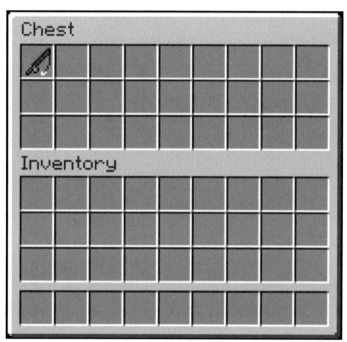

Image 17.11

Let's write a program that will make the turtle take the rod out of the chest.

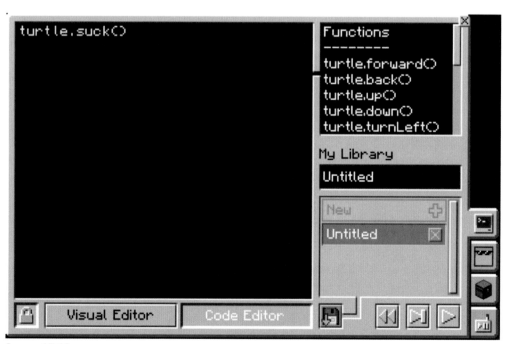

Image 17.12

After the program is executed, the fishing rod ended up in the turtle's active slot.

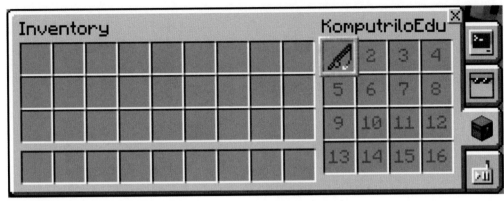

Image 17.13

Exercise 160
Place leather boots in the chest. The turtle's inventory should be empty.
Write a program that will make the turtle pull the item out of the chest and identify it (say what item is it).

Exercise 161
Place a chest in front of the turtle, and leave some empty space behind the turtle. Fill the chest up with at least 10 different blocks from the decoration blocks tab.

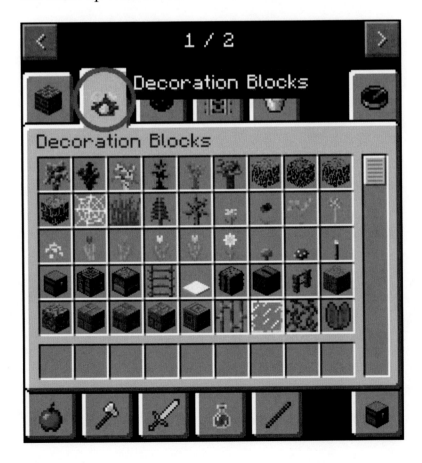

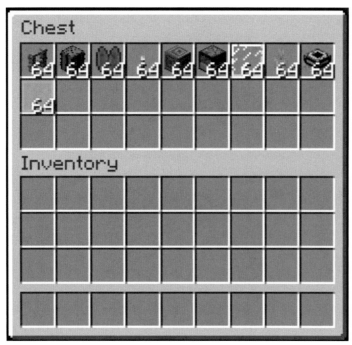

Image 17.14

Write a program that will make the turtle take one item out of the chest, turn around, throw the item behind itself, and then turn back around to the chest, repeat it ten times.

Image 17.15

Exercise 162

Place a chest and a dispenser four blocks apart. Fill the chest with snowballs. Put the turtle behind the dispenser.

Image 17.16

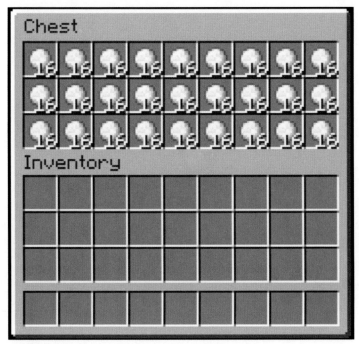

Image 17.17

Write a program that will make the turtle take a slot of snowballs from the chest to the dispenser, and then turn the dispenser on and off sixteen times.

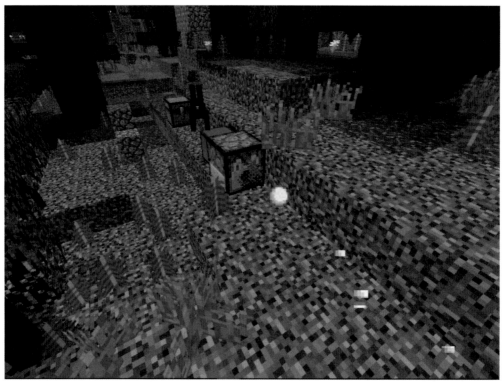

Image 17.18

Chapter 18: Summary

Sincere congratulations for finishing the second level course of coding with Minecraft. You have learned the universal concepts, knowledge of which will allow you to understand different programming languages. Remember, a programmer is always learning new things, so you always have to be improving your skills.

Image 18.11

Chapter 19: Exercise solutions

Exercise 6.

```
turtle.up()
turtle.forward()
turtle.forward()
turtle.forward()
turtle.down()
```

Image 19.1

Exercise 8.

```
turtle.turnLeft()
turtle.turnLeft()
turtle.forward()
turtle.forward()
```

Image 19.2

Exercise 9.

```
turtle.forward()
turtle.forward()
turtle.turnLeft()
turtle.forward()
turtle.forward()
turtle.turnRight()
turtle.forward()
```

Image 19.3

Exercise 10.

```
turtle.forward()
turtle.back()
turtle.up()
turtle.down()
turtle.turnLeft()
turtle.turnRight()
```

Image 19.4

Exercise 12.

```
turtle.dig()
turtle.forward()
turtle.dig()
turtle.forward()
turtle.dig()
```

Image 19.5

Exercise 13.

```
turtle.forward()
turtle.dig()
turtle.forward()
turtle.forward()
turtle.dig()
turtle.forward()
turtle.forward()
turtle.dig()
turtle.forward()
turtle.forward()
```

Image 19.6

Exercise 14.

```
turtle.forward()
turtle.up()
turtle.forward()
turtle.forward()
turtle.down()
turtle.up()
turtle.forward()
turtle.forward()
turtle.down()
turtle.up()
turtle.forward()
turtle.forward()
turtle.down()
```

Image 19.7

Exercise 15.

```
turtle.dig()
turtle.turnLeft()
turtle.dig()
turtle.turnLeft()
turtle.dig()
turtle.turnLeft()
turtle.dig()
```

Image 19.8

Exercise 16.

```
turtle.digUp()
turtle.up()
turtle.digUp()
turtle.up()
turtle.digUp()
turtle.up()
turtle.digUp()
```

Image 19.9

Exercise 17.

```
turtle.digDown()
turtle.forward()
turtle.digDown()
turtle.forward()
turtle.digDown()
turtle.forward()
turtle.digDown()
turtle.forward()
turtle.digDown()
```

Image 19.10

Exercise 18.

```
turtle.forward()
turtle.digDown()
turtle.forward()
turtle.forward()
turtle.digDown()
turtle.forward()
turtle.forward()
turtle.digDown()
```

Image 19.11

Exercise 19.

```
turtle.up()
turtle.forward()
turtle.forward()
turtle.digDown()
```

Image 19.12

Exercise 20.

```
turtle.dig()
turtle.forward()
turtle.digUp()
```

Image 19.13

Exercise 22.

```
turtle.place()
turtle.up()
turtle.place()
turtle.up()
turtle.place()
```

Image 19.14

Exercise 23.

```
turtle.place()
turtle.turnRight()
turtle.forward()
turtle.forward()
turtle.forward()
turtle.forward()
turtle.forward()
turtle.turnLeft()
turtle.place()
```

Image 19.15

Exercise 25.

```
turtle.placeUp()
turtle.digUp()
turtle.placeUp()
turtle.digUp()
```

Image 19.16

Exercise 26.

```
turtle.forward()
turtle.forward()
turtle.turnLeft()
turtle.forward()
turtle.forward()
turtle.turnLeft()
turtle.forward()
turtle.forward()
turtle.turnLeft()
turtle.forward()
turtle.forward()
```

Image 19.17

```
turtle.forward()
turtle.placeDown()
turtle.forward()
turtle.placeDown()
turtle.turnLeft()
turtle.forward()
turtle.placeDown()
turtle.forward()
turtle.placeDown()
turtle.turnLeft()
turtle.forward()
turtle.placeDown()
turtle.forward()
turtle.placeDown()
turtle.turnLeft()
turtle.forward()
turtle.placeDown()
turtle.forward()
turtle.placeDown()
```

Image 19.18

```
turtle.up()
turtle.place()
```

Image 19.19

```
turtle.forward()
turtle.digDown()
turtle.forward()
turtle.forward()
turtle.forward()
turtle.placeDown()
```

Image 19.20

```
turtle.place()
turtle.select(2)
turtle.up()
turtle.place()
turtle.select(1)
turtle.up()
turtle.place()
turtle.select(2)
turtle.up()
turtle.place()
```

Image 19.21

Exercise 31.

```
turtle.select(1)
turtle.place()
turtle.up()
turtle.forward()
turtle.select(2)
turtle.place()
turtle.up()
turtle.forward()
turtle.select(3)
turtle.place()
turtle.up()
turtle.forward()
turtle.select(1)
turtle.place()
turtle.up()
turtle.forward()
turtle.select(2)
turtle.place()
```

Image 19.22

Exercise 32.

```
turtle.place()
turtle.turnRight()
turtle.forward()
turtle.turnLeft()
turtle.place()
turtle.turnRight()
turtle.forward()
turtle.turnLeft()
turtle.select(2)
turtle.place()
turtle.turnRight()
turtle.forward()
turtle.turnLeft()
turtle.place()
```

Image 19.23

Exercise 33.

```
turtle.select(1)
turtle.dig()
turtle.forward()
turtle.select(2)
turtle.dig()
turtle.forward()
turtle.select(3)
turtle.dig()
```

Image 19.24

Exercise 34.

```
turtle.select(1)
turtle.place()
turtle.back()
turtle.select(2)
turtle.place()
turtle.select(3)
turtle.place()
```

Image 19.25

Exercise 35.

```
--jump
turtle.up()
turtle.down()
--collect block under turtle
turtle.digDown()
--place block above turtle
turtle.placeUp()
```

Image 19.26

Exercise 36.

```
turtle.place()
turtle.back()
turtle.place()
turtle.back()
turtle.place()
turtle.back()
turtle.place()
turtle.back()
turtle.place()
turtle.select(2) --Flint and Steel
turtle.up()
turtle.place()_
```

Image 19.27

Exercise 38.

1. The turtle will go forward three times.
2. The turtle will place a block once.
3. The turtle will go up three times.
4. You can replace n=1, 3 with n=1, 6

Exercise 39.

```
for n = 1, 10 do
turtle.place()
turtle.dig()
end
```

Image 19.28

Exercise 40.

```
for n = 1, 15 do
turtle.placeDown()
turtle.forward()
end
```

Image 19.29

Exercise 42.

```
for n = 1, 64 do
turtle.place()
end
```

Image 19.30

Exercise 43.

```
for n = 1, 10 do
turtle.turnRight() --Repeat
end
turtle.forward() --I do not repeat
```

Image 19.31

Exercise 44.

```
for n = 1, 6 do
turtle.placeDown()
turtle.forward()
end
turtle.select(2)
turtle.placeDown()
```

Image 19.32

Exercise 45.

```
for n = 1, 8 do
turtle.place()
turtle.up()
end
turtle.select(2)
turtle.place()
```

Image 19.33

Exercise 46.

```
turtle.placeUp()
turtleedu.say("Red")
turtle.digUp()
turtle.select(2)
turtle.placeUp()
turtleedu.say("Yellow")
turtle.digUp()
turtle.select(3)
turtle.placeUp()
turtleedu.say("Orange")
```

Image 19.34

Exercise 47.

```
for n = 1, 10 do
    turtle.forward()
    turtle.back()
    turtleedu.say("Hello, hello")
    turtle.up()
    turtle.down()
    turtleedu.say("I am so pretty")
end
```

Image 19.35

Exercise 49.

X = 3 X = X + 1	X = 4
Y = 4 Y = Y + Y	Y = 8
Z = X + Y	Z = 12
W = 9 W = W – 3	W = 6
W = W – X	W = 2
X = 3 + 1 X = X * 2	X = 8

Exercise 50.

```
number = 8
turtleedu.say(number) -- 1.
number = number + 4
turtleedu.say(number) -- 2.
number = number - 2
turtleedu.say(number) -- 3.
number = number / 2
turtleedu.say(number) -- 4.
number = number × 3
turtleedu.say(number) -- 5.
```

Image 19.36

1. 8
2. 12
3. 10
4. 5
5. 15

Exercise 52.

```
x = 20
for n = 1, 20 do
    turtleedu.say(x)
    x = x - 1
end
```

Image 19.37

Exercise 53.

```
blocks = 0
turtle.digDown()
blocks = blocks + 1
turtleedu.say(blocks)
turtle.forward()
turtle.digDown()
blocks = blocks + 1
turtleedu.say(blocks)
turtle.forward()
turtle.digDown()
blocks = blocks + 1
turtleedu.say(blocks)_
```

Image 19.38

Exercise 54.

```
water = 1
lava = 2
turtle.select(water)
turtle.placeDown()
turtle.select(lava)
turtle.placeDown()
```

Image 19.39

Exercise 56.

```
w = "Woof woof"
for n = 1, 20 do
   turtleedu.say(w)
end
turtle.place()
```

Image 19.40

Exercise 57.

```
for n = 1, 16 do
   turtleedu.say(n×2)
end
```

Image 19.41

Exercise 58.

```
for n = 1, 10 do
   turtle.select(n)
   turtle.dig()
   turtle.forward()
end
```

Image 19.42

```
for n = 1, 16 do
   turtle.select(n)
   turtle.place()
   turtle.up()
end
```

Image 19.43

Exercise 62.

6 < 2	FALSE
10 = 4	FALSE
6 = 6	TRUE
6 > 3	TRUE
3 ≠ 3	FALSE

Exercise 64.

```
turtleedu.say(3>6)
turtleedu.say(2<2)
turtleedu.say(11>=11)
turtleedu.say(4+4==40)
```

Image 19.44

Exercise 65.

```
X = 8
turtleedu.say(X==2)
```

Image 19.45

Exercise 67.

1. False
2. True
3. False
4. True
5. True
6. False!
7. True
8. Nothing, the variable is created here.
9. True

Exercise 68.

1. True
2. Won't say anything
3. False
4. True

Exercise 69.

The turtle will only jump, because 5>2 is true. The second if statement won't execute, because 6<1 is false.

Exercise 70.

You need to put "chocolate" into x.

Exercise 73.

```
turtle.select(math.random(3))
turtle.place()
turtle.up()
```

Image 19.46

Exercise 74.

```
x = math.random(3)
if x == 1 then
    turtle.placeUp()
end
if x == 2 then
    turtle.digDown()
    turtle.down()
end
if x == 3 then
    turtle.turnRight()
    turtle.turnRight()
end
```

Image 19.47

Exercise 75.

```
HP = math.random(10)
if HP < 3 then
    turtleedu.say("Low HP")
    turtle.place()
end
if HP >= 3 then
    turtle.up()
    turtle.down()
end
```

Image 19.48

Exercise 76.

```
x = math.random(2)
if x == 1 then
    turtle.select(1) --Water Bucket
    turtleedu.say("Ahoy Captain")
    turtle.place()
end
if x == 2 then
    turtle.select(2) --Painting
    turtleedu.say("I'm hiding")
    turtle.place()
end
```

Image 19.49

Exercise 77.

The turtle will start to build a snowman, because the if condition is true.

Exercise 78.

Because 1+1+1 is not equal to 2, the else code will execute.

```
x = math.random(10)
if x >= 8 then
   turtle.select(1)
   turtle.place()
   turtleedu.say("Something is wrong
else
   turtle.select(2)
   turtle.place()
end
```

Image 19.50

Exercise 81.

```
x = math.random(2)
if x == 1 then
   for n = 1, 100 do
      turtle.forward()
   end
else
   for n = 1, 100 do
      turtle.up()
   end
end
```

Image 19.51

Exercise 83.

```
for n = 1, 20 do
   if n < 15 then
      turtle.select(1)
      turtle.place()
   else
      turtle.select(2)
      turtle.place()
   end
end
```

Image 19.52

Exercise 84.

Carrot = false Melon = true	The turtle will plant melons
Carrot = true Melon = true	The turtle will plant carrots
Carrot = true Melon = false	The turtle will plant carrots
Carrot = false Melon = false	The turtle won't plant anything

Exercise 85.

1. The turtle will dig a block.
2. The turtle will turn right.
3. The turtle will dig down.
4. The turtle will say "Banana".

Exercise 86.

```
X = math.random(3)
if X == 1 then
    turtleedu.say("I am a shepherd")
elseif X == 2 then
    turtle.up()
    turtle.up()
else
    turtle.placeDown()
end
```

Image 19.53

Exercise 87.

```
X = math.random(10)
if X <= 3 then
    turtle.select(1)
    turtle.place()
elseif X <= 6 then
    turtle.select(2)
    turtle.place()
else
    turtle.select(3)
    turtle.place()
end
```

Image 19.54

Exercise 88.

```
for n = 1, 12 do
    if n < 5 then
        turtleedu.say(n)
    elseif n < 10 then
        turtle.up()
        turtle.place()
    else
        turtle.down()
        turtle.down()
        turtle.dig()
    end
end
```

Image 19.55

Exercise 89.

If — If something is true, execute the code.

Elseif — Else if the previous condition is false but this one is true, execute another code fragment.

Else — Else, when all the conditions are false, execute a different code fragment.

Exercise 90.
1. Yes
2. No
3. Yes

Exercise 91.
1. Yes
2. No
3. Yes

Exercise 92.
1. No
2. Yes
3. Yes

Exercise 94.

Turns around	1, 2, 8, 9
Goes one block up	3, 6
Places a block under itself	4
Does nothing	5, 7

Exercise 95.

```
for n = 1, 50 do
   turtle.place()
   turtle.dig()
end
```

Image 19.56

Exercise 97.

```
if turtleedu.checkRedstone() then
   turtle.placeUp()
else
   turtle.forward()
end
```

Image 19.57

Exercise 98.

```
if turtleedu.checkRedstone() then
   for n = 1, 10 do
      turtle.digDown()
      turtle.down()
   end
else
   for n = 1, 20 do
      turtle.digDown()
      turtle.down()
   end
end
```

Image 19.58

Exercise 100.

```
if turtleedu.checkRedstoneUp() then
    turtle.digUp()
end
```

Image 19.59

Exercise 102.

```
if turtleedu.checkRedstoneDown() then
    turtleedu.say(math.random(1, 100))
end
```

Image 19.60

Exercise 104.

```
X = 0
if turtleedu.checkRedstone() then
    X = X + 1
end
if turtleedu.checkRedstoneUp() then
    X = X + 2
end
if turtleedu.checkRedstoneDown() then
    X = X + 4
end
turtleedu.say(X)
```

Image 19.61

When you activate the redstone dust above and behind the turtle, it will display 6, because 2 + 4 = 6.

Exercise 106.

```
for n = 1, 20 do
    turtleedu.setRedstone(true)
    turtleedu.setRedstone(false)
end
```

Image 19.62

Exercise 107.

```
if turtleedu.checkRedstoneDown() then
    turtleedu.setRedstone(true)
    turtleedu.setRedstone(false)
end
```

Image 19.63

Exercise 108.

```
turtle.place()
turtle.back()
turtle.place()
turtleedu.setRedstone(true)
```

Image 19.64

Exercise 109.

```
turtle.placeUp()
turtleedu.setRedstoneUp(true)
turtle.digDown()
turtle.down()
turtle.digDown()
turtle.down()
turtle.select(2)
turtle.placeUp()
```

Image 19.65

Exercise 110.

```
for n = 1, 64 do
   turtleedu.setRedstone(true)
   turtleedu.setRedstone(false)
end
```

Image 19.66

Exercise 111.

```
for n = 1, 50 do
   X = math.random(3)
   if X == 1 then
     turtleedu.setRedstone(true)
     turtleedu.setRedstone(false)
   elseif X == 2 then
     turtleedu.setRedstoneUp(true)
     turtleedu.setRedstoneUp(false)
   else
     turtleedu.setRedstoneDown(true)
     turtleedu.setRedstoneDown(false)
   end
end
```

Image 19.67

Exercise 113.

```
while turtleedu.checkRedstoneDown() do
   turtle.place()
   turtle.up()
end
```

Image 19.68

Exercise 115.

```
while turtleedu.checkRedstoneUp() do
   turtleedu.setRedstone(true)
   turtleedu.setRedstoneDown(true)
   turtleedu.setRedstone(false)
   turtleedu.setRedstoneDown(false)
end
```

Image 19.69

Exercise 118.

```
while true do
   X = math.random( 2 )
   if X == 1 then
      turtle.place()
      turtle.dig()
   else
      turtleedu.say("Enjoy your meal"
   end
end_
```

Image 19.70

Exercise 119.

```
while true do
   turtle.forward()
   turtle.forward()
   turtle.up()
   turtle.up()
   turtle.back()
   turtle.back()
   turtle.down()
   turtle.down()
end
```

Image 19.71

Exercise 121.

```
while true do
   turtle.forward()
   if turtle.detect() then
      turtle.dig()
   end
end
```

Image 19.72

Exercise 122.

```
while not turtle.detect() do
   turtle.placeDown()
   turtle.forward()
end
```

Image 19.73

Exercise 123.

```
while true do
   if turtle.detect() then
      turtleedu.say("I don't see")
   end
end
```

Image 19.74

Exercise 124.

```
while true do
  if turtle.detect() then
    turtle.dig()
    turtleedu.say("+1 Cobblestone")
  end
end
```

Image 19.75

Exercise 126.

```
if turtle.detectUp() then
  turtle.back()
  turtle.up()
  turtle.up()
  turtle.forward()
end
```

Image 19.76

Exercise 127.

```
if turtle.detect() then
  turtle.dig()
  turtle.place()
  turtleedu.setRedstone(true)
elseif turtle.detectDown() then
  turtle.digDown()
  turtle.down()
elseif turtle.detectUp() then
  X = math.random(80)
  turtleedu.say(X)
end
```

Image 19.77

Exercise 128.

Of course not. The conditions for those directions would have to be false, before the turtle reaches the code fragment that displays the random number.

Exercise 130.

```
piec = "minecraft:furnace"
if turtleedu.inspect() == piec then
  turtle.turnRight()
  turtle.forward()
  turtle.turnLeft()
  turtle.place()
end
```

Image 19.78

Exercise 131.

```
I = "minecraft:iron_block"
while not(turtleedu.inspect()==I) d
    turtleedu.say("eat")
end
turtleedu.say("Healthy iron")
```

Image 19.79

Exercise 132.

```
F = "minecraft:bed"
while not(turtleedu.inspect()==F) d
    turtle.turnRight()
end
```

Image 19.80

Exercise 134.

```
bottom = turtleedu.inspectDown()
top = turtleedu.inspectUp()
if bottom == top then
    turtleedu.say("Same blocks")
end
```

Image 19.81

Exercise 135.

```
for n = 1, 10 do
    Block = turtleedu.inspectDown()
    turtleedu.say(Block)
    turtle.forward()
end
```

Image 19.82

Exercise 137.

```
X = turtle.getItemCount()
turtleedu.say(math.random(X))
```

Image 19.83

Exercise 138.

```
while turtle.getItemCount() < 10 do
    turtle.dig()
    turtle.forward()
end
turtleedu.say("finished")
```

Image 19.84

Exercise 139.

```
while turtle.getItemCount() > 0 do
    turtle.placeDown()
    turtle.forward()
end
```

Image 19.85

Exercise 142.

```
for n = 1, 10 do
   turtleedu.say(n)
   os.sleep(1)
end
```

Image 19.86

Exercise 143.

```
while true do
   turtleedu.say("Horse for sale")
   os.sleep(10)
end
```

Image 19.87

Exercise 144.

```
while true do
   turtleedu.setRedstone(true)
   os.sleep(1)
   turtleedu.setRedstone(false)
   os.sleep(1)
end
```

Image 19.88

Exercise 145.

```
os.sleep(turtle.getItemCount())
turtle.place()
turtleedu.setRedstone(true)
```

Image 19.89

Exercise 147.

```
for n = 1, 16 do
   turtle.select(n)
   Item = turtleedu.getItemName()
   turtleedu.say(Item)
end
```

Image 19.90

Exercise 148.

```
Item = turtleedu.getItemName()
while not(Item=="minecraft:diamond_
   turtle.select(math.random(16))
   Item = turtleedu.getItemName()
end
turtleedu.say("I'm going to fight")
```

Image 19.91

Exercise 149.

```
for n = 1, 16 do
   turtle.select(n)
   if turtleedu.inspect() == turtlee
      turtleedu.say("I have it in my
   end
end
```

Image 19.92

Exercise 152.

```
while true do
   X = math.random(16)
   turtle.transferTo(X)
   turtle.select(X)
end
```

Image 19.93

Exercise 153.

```
gold = "minecraft:gold_ingot"
for n = 1, 16 do
   turtle.select(n)
   if turtleedu.getItemName()==gold
      turtle.transferTo(1)
   end
end
```

Image 19.94

Exercise 156.

```
while true do
   if turtle.getItemCount()>0 then
      turtle.drop()
   end
end
```

Image 19.95

Exercise 157.

```
for n = 1, 10 do
   turtle.digDown()
   turtle.down()
end
for n = 1, 10 do
   turtle.up()
end
turtle.drop()
```

Image 19.96

Exercise 158.

```
turtle.place()
turtle.up()
turtle.place()
turtle.up()
turtle.place()
turtle.down()
turtle.down()
turtle.turnLeft()
turtle.turnLeft()
turtle.drop()
```

Image 19.97

Exercise 160.

```
turtle.suck()
Item = turtleedu.getItemName()
turtleedu.say(Item)
```

Image 19.98

Exercise 161.

```
for n = 1, 10 do
   turtle.suck()
   turtle.turnLeft()
   turtle.turnLeft()
   turtle.drop()
   turtle.turnLeft()
   turtle.turnLeft()
end
```

Image 19.99

Exercise 162.

```
turtle.turnLeft()
turtle.turnLeft()
turtle.forward()
turtle.forward()
turtle.forward()
turtle.suck()
turtle.turnLeft()
turtle.turnLeft()
turtle.forward()
turtle.forward()
turtle.forward()
turtle.drop()
for n = 1, 16 do
   turtleedu.setRedstone(true)
   turtleedu.setRedstone(false)
end
```

Image 19. 100

Your list of completed tasks

Task number	Is it solved?
1	
2	
3	
4	
5	
6	
7	
8	
9	
10	
11	
12	
13	
14	
15	
16	
17	
18	
19	
20	
21	
22	
23	
24	
25	
26	
27	
28	
29	
30	
31	
32	
33	
34	
35	
36	
37	
38	
39	
40	
41	
42	
43	
44	
45	
46	
47	
48	
49	
50	
51	
52	
53	

54	
55	
56	
57	
58	
59	
60	
61	
62	
63	
64	
65	
66	
67	
68	
69	
70	
71	
72	
73	
74	
75	
76	
77	
78	
79	
80	
81	
82	
83	
84	
85	
86	
87	
88	
89	
90	
91	
92	
93	
94	
95	
96	
97	
98	
99	
100	
101	
102	
103	
104	
105	
106	
107	
108	

109	
110	
111	
112	
113	
114	
115	
116	
117	
118	
119	
120	
121	
122	
123	
124	
125	
126	
127	
128	
129	
130	
131	
132	
133	
134	
135	
136	
137	
138	
139	
140	
141	
142	
143	
144	
145	
146	
147	
148	
149	
150	
151	
152	
153	
154	
155	
156	
157	
158	
159	
160	
161	
162	
Congratulations!	

Made in the USA
Middletown, DE
08 December 2020